An Environmental Agenda for the Future

John H. Adams
Natural Resources Defense Council

Louise C. Dunlap
Environmental Policy Institute

Jay D. Hair
National Wildlife Federation

Frederick D. Krupp
Environmental Defense Fund

Jack Lorenz
The Izaak Walton League of America

J. Michael McCloskey
Sierra Club

Russell W. Peterson
National Audubon Society

Paul C. Pritchard
National Parks and Conservation Association

William A. Turnage
The Wilderness Society

Karl Wendelowski
Friends of the Earth

Names of organizations for identification purposes only.

ISLAND PRESS
Washington, D.C. • Covelo, CA

PUBLISHED BY ISLAND PRESS, a nonprofit conservation organization dedicated to the distribution and publication of books for professionals and concerned citizens at work on the conservation and management of natural resources and the environment.

Funds to support ISLAND PRESS and the publication of this book were provided by the Donner Foundation, the Ford Foundation, the Joint Foundation Support, the Rockefeller Brothers' Fund and the Tides Foundation.

ISLAND PRESS 1718 Connecticut Avenue, NW Suite 300, Washington, D.C. 20009. ISLAND PRESS Star Route 1, Box 38, Covelo, CA 95428.

Island Press edition published by arrangement with Agenda Press.

Library of Congress Cataloging in Publication Data

An Environmental Agenda for the Future

    Bibliography: p. 149
       1. Environmental protection—United States
2. Conservation of Natural Resources—United States
I. Adams, John H. (John Hamilton), 1936- . II. Cahn, Robert, 1917- .
TD171.E56 1985   304.2   85-19760
ISBN 0-933280-29-7 (pbk.)

Printed in the United States.

An Environmental
Agenda
for the Future

Contents

Acknowledgments

The authors of this book gratefully acknowledge the assistance of the many individuals who have contributed their time and expertise during the two-year span of the project.

A first word of appreciation goes to Russell W. Peterson and J. Michael McCloskey of our group of chief executive officers, who originated the concept of developing an environmental agenda for the future. Peterson, as chairman of the agenda project, guided the effort to completion. An indispensable influence throughout was Robert L. Allen of the Henry P. Kendall Foundation, who gave his personal interest and commitment to the agenda. Special thanks also go to two others who were the chief executive officers of their organizations when the project began and who made a substantial contribution to it during 1983 and 1984—Rafe Pomerance of Friends of the Earth and Janet Brown of the Environmental Defense Fund. Others giving their expertise were Robert Chlopak, Acting Executive Director of Friends of the Earth during the latter part of 1984, and Allen E. Smith, President of Defenders of Wildlife.

For coordination of the project and editorial direction from January 1985 to completion, we thank Robert Cahn of National Audubon Society and also gratefully acknowledge the editorial work donated by Patricia L. Cahn. Joanne Lavelle, Beth Spencer, and Monica Wells of National Wildlife Federation assisted with their word processing skills. Wayne E. Nail, Natural Resources Defense Council, designed and coordinated production of this book.

The chief executive officers who worked together in developing this environmental agenda also express their appreciation to the W. Alton Jones Foundation, the Ruth Mott Fund, The George Gund Foundation, and Ted and Jennifer Stanley for their generous support of the project and its publication. The authors wish to make clear that the donors are not in any way responsible for the content of this publication.

Invaluable advice and supporting data came from eleven task forces.

The Nuclear Issues Task force, chaired by Rafe Pomerance and coordinated by David Lewis of Friends of the Earth, included Robert Alvarez, Environmental Policy Institute; Robert Cahn; David Burwell, National Wildlife Federation; with assistance from Estelle Rogers and Barbara Finamore, Natural Resources Defense Council; Chaplin Barnes and Jacob Scherr, Center on the Consequences of Nuclear War; and Jeremy Stone, Federation of American Scientists.

The Human Population Issues task force, chaired by Russell W. Peterson and coordinated by the late Frances Breed, National Audubon Society, included David Chatfield, Friends of the Earth; Judy Kunofsky, Sierra Club; and Richard Beamish and Jodi Jacobsen, National Audubon Society; with assistance from Philander P. Claxton, Jr., World Population Society.

The Energy Strategies task force, chaired by Louise Dunlap and coordinated by Keiki Kehoe, Environmental Policy Institute, included Jan Beyea, National Audubon Society; Alden Meyer, Environmental Action; Norman Dean, National Wildlife Federation; Florentine Krause, Friends of the Earth; and David Roe, Environmental Defense Fund; with assistance from William U. Chandler, Worldwatch Institute.

The Water Resources task force, chaired by Jack Lorenz and coordinated by Maitland Sharp, The Izaak Walton League of America, included Brent Blackwelder and Pete Carlson, Environmental Policy Institute; David Conrad, Friends of the Earth; Tom Graff, Environmental Defense Fund; and Ed Osann, National Wildlife Federation.

The Toxics and Pollution task force, chaired by John H. Adams and coordinated by Jonathan Lash, Natural Resources Defense Council, included Leslie Dach, National Audubon Society; Blake Early, Sierra Club; Ken Kamlet, National Wildlife Federation; John McCormick, Environmental Policy Institute; Robert Percival, Environmental Defense Fund; Marchant Wentworth, The Izaak Walton League of America; and Richard Ayers and Melissa Paly, Natural Resources Defense Council; with assistance from Frederic D. Krupp.

The Wild Living Resources task force, chaired and coordinated by Michael Bean, Environmental Defense Fund, included Faith Campbell, Natural Resources Defense Council; Amos Eno, National Audubon Society; Lynn Greenwalt and Alan Wentz, National Wildlife Federation; Laura Loomis, National Parks and Conservation Association; and Elizabeth Raisbeck, Friends of the Earth; with assistance from Jay Copeland, National Audubon Society.

The Private Lands and Agriculture task force, chaired by Paul Pritchard and coordinated by William Lienesch, National Parks and Conservation Association, included Maureen Hinkle, National Audubon Society; Justin Ward, Natural Resources Defense Council; Rose McCullough, Sierra Club; Robert Pierce, National Parks and Conservation Association; Elizabeth Raisbeck; and Jack Doyle, Environmental Policy Institute; with assistance from William Shands, The Conservation Foundation; Gaylord Nelson and Peter Kirby, The Wilderness Society; Robert Davison, National Wildlife Federation; and Kevin Coyle and Malcolm Baldwin, American Land Resource Association.

The Protected Land Systems task force, chaired by William A. Turnage and coordinated by Charles Clusen and Deanne Kloepfer, The Wilderness Society, included Brent Blackwelder; Laura Beaty, National Parks and Conservation Association; David Conrad; and John McComb, Sierra Club; with assistance from Clay Peters and William Reffalt, The Wilderness Society; and Allen E. Smith.

The Public Lands task force, chaired by J. Michael McCloskey and coordinated by Bruce Hamilton, Sierra Club, included Andrew Palmer, Environmental Policy Institute; Trent Orr, Natural Resources Defense Council; Peter Kirby; and Geoff Webb, Friends of the Earth; with assistance from Philip Hocker, Sierra Club.

The Urban Environment task force, chaired by John H. Adams and coordinated by Eric A. Goldstein, Natural Resources Defense Council, included Pete Lafen, Friends of the Earth; Norris McDonald, Environmental Policy Institute; Jim Tripp, Environmental Defense Fund; and Melissa Paly; with assistance from Sydney Howe, Human Environment Center.

The International Issues task force, chaired by Russell W. Peterson and coordinated by Robert Cahn, included Barbara Bramble, National Wildlife Federation; David Chatfield; Frances Lipscomb, National Audubon Society; Andrew Palmer; Pat Scharlin, Sierra Club; and Thomas Stoel, Natural Resources Defense Council; with assistance from Lee Talbot, World Resources Institute; Joan M. Nicholson, United Nations Environment Programme; Lester R. Brown, Worldwatch Institute; Michael Wright, World Wildlife Fund; Clif Curtis, Oceanic Society; David Runnals, International Institute for Environment and Development; and James N. Barnes, Antarctic and Southern Ocean Coalition.

Those who helped with the Background and Synopsis of the Issues included David Burwell, National Wildlife Federation; Robert Percival; Thomas Stoel and Robert Hamrin, Natural Resources Defense Council; Edwin H. Clark, II, The Conservation Foundation; Joseph Browder, Washington, D.C., and Robert L. Allen.

Others giving information and assistance during the project included Frances Dubrowski, Natural Resources Defense Council; Ed Norton The Wilderness Society; John Gibbons, Office of Technology Assessment; Sidney D. Drell, Stanford University; Fritjof Capra, Lawrence Berkeley Laboratory; Amos Funk, Millersville, Pennsylvania; Eugene A. Nida, Greenwich, Connecticut; Marieluise Beck-Oberdorf, Bonn, West Germany; Douglas M. Costle, Washington, D.C.; Michele A. Tingling, Association of Community Organizations for Reform Now; and Peter S. Thacher, World Resources Institute.

Background and Synopsis of the Issues

Introduction

Early in 1981, we, the chief executives of 10 major environmental and conservation organizations, began meeting informally to enhance our effectiveness in helping to protect the nation's environmental quality. The idea of setting out an agenda for the future began to take shape two years ago at a suggestion that we step back and think about where the environmental movement should be going and what goals it should be pursuing. We realized that in addition to defending the many environmental gains of recent years, we needed to look beyond the current legislative docket and budget battles to problems and opportunities out to the end of the century and beyond. We also recognized that solutions to emerging environmental problems require a public dialogue on the nature and dimensions of the challenges, and that in light of political, social, and technological trends, a successful strategy for the future must appeal to the broadest spectrum of the American people. We hope that this look at the larger picture will spawn fresh ways of thinking and new ideas to help in the pursuit of environmental quality.

This agenda for the future has roots deep in the American tradition of citizen action. We are sincerely asking for the help of all concerned people. We feel that success in the coming years depends on a framework that defines public environmental needs, offers guidelines for channeling public energies in positive ways, and facilitates public participation at every level. In developing the agenda, we tapped the experience of our most knowledgeable senior staff members and drew upon the expertise of people representing more than a dozen other environmental, population, and public interest organizations.

While our informal group reflects the diversity of today's environmental movement, our agenda is by no means an attempt to speak for the movement as a whole. Rather, through informal collaboration, it presents a consensus among a representative cross-section of conservation leaders. It will be obvious to readers of this document that the common objective is to protect and enhance the quality of life worldwide. The focus is not to predict the future, but to address the future by formulation of possible courses toward that goal, which all of us share, of a sustainable society and a better quality of life, to accept obligations to set a responsible example, and to work with other countries throughout the world in meeting global problems.

Background

For more than a century Americans, as individuals and as part of what has grown into a nationwide conservation movement, have been a motivating force behind the formulation and implementation of public conservation policies. In the early days it was a small group of wilderness-loving citizens who decided that the Yellowstone area should be preserved for posterity, and succeeded in having Congress establish it as the world's first national park in 1872 "for the benefit and enjoyment of the people." To achieve their objectives, hunters, fishermen, and outdoorsmen, forest conservators, bird protectors, and wilderness advocates formed organizations, each with a particular motivation for saving the nation's natural resources and scenic beauty. Thus were the roots of the conservation movement formed in the 19th and early 20th centuries.

By the 1950s the challenges had changed and multiplied. The pressures of a burgeoning population led to a passion for acquisition and development of land and resources that overtook the nation. Decades of overuse and inappropriate use had contaminated lakes, rivers, and streams; city air was heavy with pollution; sewage and solid waste were fouling population centers; and many of the nation's last remaining wilderness areas were threatened by exploitation. DDT, originally hailed as a great benefactor, was discovered to have dangerous side effects as it worked its way through the food chain, weakening and killing wildlife, and posing serious threats to human health. Within a few years hundreds of other substances were found to be detrimental to human health.

In the face of these and other threats, the conservation movement had to redefine its purposes. The old concept of conservation as the "wise use" of natural resources—rivers to be dammed for irrigation and hydropower or forests used primarily as sources of timber—were not sufficient for the needs of the times. The old priorities had to be reconsidered in line with other factors such as the intrinsic value of the rivers, oceans, and forests, the land and the atmosphere, habitat for the wildlife, sustainable ecological systems, and places for harmonious living, recreation, and aesthetic opportunity.

In the 1960s and 1970s, these new concerns coalesced into an environmental revolution. By Earth Day 1970, the stalwarts of the conservation community were joined by millions of people acutely aware of the state of their environment and its potential effects on the health and well-being of their families and neighbors. They were women and men, young and old, poor and wealthy—homemakers, students, people from the professions, business, and labor, all reacting to what they saw happening to the air, the water, and the land. Political leaders who had not shown much concern for environmental affairs suddenly responded to the will of the people. At the start of the '70s, a President sent to Congress three consecutive annual environmental messages outlining the legislation being demanded by the American public. Congress enacted laws for stricter regulations on air and water pollution, to reduce solid waste, prevent ocean dumping, restrict harmful pesticides, require reclamation of lands stripmined for coal, and control toxic wastes, to add wilderness, wildlife refuges, and national parks, protect wetlands, coastal areas, and endangered species, and to assist in providing more urban and state parks and outdoor recreation. And at the end of the decade, Congress acted to protect for the entire nation and future generations most of the still pristine Alaska federal lands.

The agenda of the '70s was reactive to a newly perceived crisis. The laws and regulations met with resistance, however, and compliance had to be won through citizen vigilance and court actions. The National Environmental Policy Act of 1969 (NEPA) set forth a continuing policy for the federal government, as a trustee of the environment for succeeding generations, to "attain the widest range of beneficial uses of the environment without degradation, risk to health or safety, or other undesirable and unintended consequences" and to "achieve a balance between population and resource use which will permit high standards of living and a wide sharing of life's amenities." To implement this policy, the law required all agencies of the federal government to prepare environmental impact statements before making any proposal for legislation and other major federal action that could significantly affect the quality of the human environment.

Problems of the Future

Marked progress has been made in the 16 years since passage of NEPA, but many of the problems it was meant to solve still remain. Congress has passed a multitude of laws, and the courts have in many instances upheld the lawsuits brought by citizens to force compliance by some recalcitrant elements in industry and government agencies. But compliance and enforcement are still spotty and not adequately achieving the purposes of the laws. And because the laws and regulations often have not dealt with root causes, they have been inadequate to cope with added problems that have arisen, partly from new technologies.

Many of today's problems are global in scope and make local, regional, or even national solutions difficult. These problems include human population growth that is exceeding the capacity of some countries to feed and sustain their burgeoning numbers; toxic chemicals, developed with the intent of benefiting humankind, that turn out to be serious threats to health with side effects that kill and maim; the greatly increased burning of fossil fuels, producing atmospheric effects that could melt icecaps and flood coastal cities. Looming over all is the specter of nuclear war with its massive immediate death and destruction, which could be followed by the cold and dark of nuclear winter spreading climatic change throughout the world, destroying the life support systems, eliminating many species of plants and animals, and even threatening the survival of the human species.

These and other global problems call for pragmatic approaches and an agenda that can help the nation look toward ways of meeting the environmental challenges of the next 15 years and on into the new century. Building upon the strategies that have brought results in the past two decades, citizens, working with government, must continue to find new ways to achieve solutions.

The Economy-Environment Link

The increased visibility of citizen and governmental efforts to meet environmental challenges in the past two decades has stimulated debate about how concern for the environment affects other important national objectives, particularly economic ones. When there is conflict over objectives, various interests predictably bring different perspectives to the role environmental concerns have in shaping other important national goals. Some public officials and business executives have suggested that environmental regulations are strangling business and industry and have sought to weaken or abolish the environmental protection laws enacted in the 1960s and 1970s.

The public and many economists, however, do not give credence to that argument. When a recent Gallup poll asked citizens what they would do if they had to choose between economic growth or environmental protection, the citizens, two-to-one, favored protecting the environment. Numerous economic analyses have shown that such a choice does not need to be made because no inevitable significant conflict exists between economic strength and environmental protection.

Concern for the environment at a deeply personal level has joined with concern for economic well-being and the two have become integrated into a quality-of-life goal shared by Americans from all regions and in all economic groups. This strong public support is founded on the rejection of policies that would require fundamental tradeoffs of environmental quality for economic opportunity, because the majority of citizens and economists perceive that such tradeoffs are not necessary and are not likely to happen on any scale that would negatively impact on the economy. Whenever a region, an industry, or an enterprise is required to pay the cost of preventing or repairing environmental damage, or to forego the profit of developing a resource, some kinds of economic activity may become less rewarding. At the same time, new or modified enterprises may become more profitable. Americans as a people have prospered from economic change, are proud of turning challenges into rewarding opportunities, and believe that American ingenuity can solve most difficult problems. Their willingness to pay for protecting the environment is based on the assumption that the price is worth paying and will be balanced by gains in environmental quality.

More and more businesses have come to accept the fact that concern for the environment should be integrated into the planning of every resource-using enterprise. There will continue to be debate about how best to manage the nation's resources and protect the environment, but many leaders of U.S. business, industry, and labor are working creatively toward environmentally sound practices. Further, American industry has demonstrated that technological or process changes designed to protect resources can also represent sound business opportunities. For some electric utilities, investments in energy conservation and diverse, small-scale energy technologies have become attractive alternatives to traditional central-station power generation. Redesign of industrial processes and products to save energy has also saved money for producers and consumers. Integrated pest management and better irrigation technologies are saving money for many farmers. Increasingly, environmentally sound practices are being seen as good for business.

As more is learned about what must be done to protect public health and the environment, as various non-environmental factors make some industries vulnerable to added costs, and as economic and social changes make some former practices in the use of resources unacceptable, a few communities suffer economic disruption. Companies that were only marginally profitable for reasons other than pollution may be forced to close because they cannot afford to comply with pollution control laws. But poisoning the air and water, ruining land, damaging the health and safety of workers and nearby communities, or destroying wildlife and natural areas would make *sustainable* development impossible. The public's faith in society's ability to reconcile environmental and economic goals requires those working for sound resource management to be sensitive to the local or temporary negative economic implications that can result from some environmental policy choices. In those instances when the national interest requires environmental protection measures that do result in some degree of local or regional economic dislocation, industry and government working together should provide help for affected communities and families.

There is ample evidence that sound resource management and careful protection of the environment are necessary to American society and of value to the economy. From the human tragedy of the 1930s dustbowl, when the rural U.S. heartland paid for years of abusive soil management, to more recent examples of fisheries closed in Virginia's James River because of Kepone, or communities abandoned in Love Canal, New York, and

Times Beach, Missouri because of irresponsible hazardous waste management, failure to protect the environment has disrupted lives and cost billions of dollars.

Benefits of Regulation

Economists and most business executives recognize that prevention is cheaper in the long run than the costs of cleaning up pollution. The economic benefits accruing from laws or regulations established to prevent or avoid environmental harm are sometimes difficult to quantify. These benefits include fewer medical bills, less time off work due to illness, reduced property damage, and increased crop yields. Also the necessity of preventing pollution or cleaning it up has led to development of new industrial processes and served to increase economic efficiency.

Continued economic growth is essential. Past environmental gains will be maintained and new ones made more easily in a healthy economy than in a stagnant one with continued high unemployment. Subsidies that stimulate harm to the environment should be removed and the government should charge realistic prices for publicly owned natural resources. Laws and regulations adopted to protect the environment should be formulated, whenever possible, so as to give manufacturers a continuing incentive to protect the environment as part of making a profit. Competitive pressures will, however, lead businesses to develop more efficient and less costly processes that prevent environmental harm.

One of the problems in relating economic health and environmental health is that the nation has not developed a quality of life index that measures both. Environmental health factors such as morbidity and mortality, crop and forest damage, soil erosion, air and water pollution, and aesthetic degradation are given little attention compared to such economic health factors as Gross National Product (GNP) and unemployment. Much work needs to be done to develop and use more comprehensive measurements of quality of life.

The relationship between economic prosperity and environmental health extends far beyond U.S. borders. In a global economy, the United States has a direct economic interest in the environmental quality and resource management practices of the rest of the world, and vice versa. Apart from all countries' obvious common concern about the oceans and the atmosphere and the imperative need to prevent the ultimate human and environmental tragedy of nuclear war, it is becoming ever more apparent that the United States will not prosper if global biological systems become more abused. The economic consequences of desertification in Mexico or Africa are felt in the United States. Manufacture of American goods overseas in areas requiring minimal pollution control or safety measures costs Americans jobs. And when this practice leads to the perception of American responsibility for lost lives, damaged health, or degraded communities, the direct and indirect costs can be severe. American economic relations with other nations should include encouragement of sound resource management and environmental protection, with emphasis on restoration of fisheries, soils, and forests.

The Issues in Brief

This agenda is not the work of a few moments. It has been two years in the making and reflects the thoughts and concerns of a good many environmental, population, and natural resource experts from many organizations. It has also drawn on ideas generated at nine regional environmental conferences held around the nation over the past four years. The Environmental Agenda for the Future is organized around 11 major subject areas: 1. nuclear issues; 2. human population growth; 3. energy strategies; 4. water resources; 5. toxics and pollution control; 6. wild living resources; 7. private lands and agriculture; 8. protected land systems; 9. public lands; 10. urban environment; and 11. international responsibilities. They are summarized briefly here. More complete discussion of the issues and recommendations is presented in the chapters that follow.

Nuclear Issues

Mankind has the power to destroy all life on earth. That power may be released at any time, for it is harnessed only by fallible humans, and, increasingly, by fallible machines. As knowledge and anxiety about nuclear risks increase, however, the situation becomes impossible to ignore and difficult to tolerate. Recent scientific study has revealed that our planet is even more fragile and our "security" systems much more deadly than previously thought. Scientific findings indicate that the detonation of even a small fraction of the weapons in the world's nuclear arsenals could send enough dust and soot into the atmosphere to trigger major climatic disruptions and create a deadly, global "nuclear winter." The consequent disruptions of ecosystems could cause the extinction of many forms of life, and, some scientists believe, the extinction of the human species.

The nuclear winter studies have underscored the catastrophic consequences of nuclear war to all forms of life on earth, and have confirmed in a compelling and unavoidable way that nuclear war is the ultimate environmental threat. The President, relevant executive agencies, and the Congress should rigorously re-evaluate nuclear weapons, arms control, and civil defense policies and programs in light of the nuclear winter findings, and encourage full public review and debate of nuclear winter policy implications.

Environmental and economic costs of constructing and maintaining nuclear weapons arsenals are increasingly severe for the United States, the Soviet Union, and all nuclear nations. Proliferation of nuclear weapons greatly multiplies the environmental dangers associated with weapons production, especially for millions of people living near weapons plants. Conscience requires that action on nuclear issues be elevated to high urgency on the environmental agenda.

Education efforts in the United States should be expanded to explain the findings on nuclear winter and its implications for nuclear strategy and arms control policy. Citizens throughout the country are beginning to understand that nuclear weapons production is a threat to the health of workers in the plants, people in nearby communities, and the environment. The nuclear weapons industry should be required to internalize all the costs of nuclear weapons production and testing and comply with the same strong human health and safety regulations that govern the nuclear power industry.

To reduce the threat of nuclear war, cut down on the damages to the environment and to health from nuclear weapons production, and eventually halt the arms race, Congress should call for a mutual and verifiable moratorium, to be negotiated by the United States, the Soviet Union, and other nuclear nations, on the testing, production, and deployment of nuclear weapons, which public opinion polls show is advocated by a majority of U.S. citizens. (See Chapter 2 for other recommendations and discussion of nuclear issues.)

Human Population Growth

The 4.8 billion humans who now people the earth are overtaxing the capacities of some of the world's biological systems to support them, and are in fact reducing the earth's productive resource base at the very time when still more resources will be required to take care of the growing population. At the present rate of growth, more than six billion people will be living on earth by the year 2000.

The Third World is experiencing the highest rate of population growth. Almost half of the world's people live in the rural areas of developing countries. Their daily needs for fuel and nourishment lead them to cut the trees and bushes for firewood and then cultivate ever higher on hillsides to grow food, causing their hillside soils to wash away. They overfish and overhunt and let their domestic animals overgraze, reducing the grassy dry-lands to desert.

The United States feels the effects of global population expansion. The growing number of people and faltering economies in Latin America are causing an unprecedented amount of illegal immigration, substantially raising U.S. population. Over-cutting of tropical forests puts additional pressure on U.S. forests to fill wood product demands, and threatens plant and animal species in the tropical countries. Loss of the forests could also cause global climatic changes. Population expansion in the Middle East exacerbates that area's ethnic, religious, and political turmoil, thus heightening the possibility of interruptions in the world's access to Middle East oil reserves, with a consequent increase in the danger of Soviet-U.S. military confrontation. Population growth in Africa aggravates the already tragic problem of inadequate food production that cannot feed the starving people.

U.S. population growth results in pressures on water supplies, more air and water pollution, and destruction of wetlands and farmlands for development, and leads to overintensive farming with its resultant soil erosion.

Although 47 developing countries have adopted population programs, the rate of progress is not sufficient, nor has international assistance kept pace with the need. The Administration recently reversed the United States role and vacated the position of leadership in this area by withholding support of the two most effective international family planning organizations. Congress should reverse that policy.

The annual U.S. appropriation for international population programs should be increased, not reduced, and a higher percentage of foreign aid should go to family planning. Other governments should also increase their support. All economic assistance programs of the U.S. Agency for International Development should include family planning, and the World Bank and other international funding institutions should give increased priority to population stabilization. Without substantial increases in funds for family planning, the developing world is doomed to repeat endlessly the tragedy unfolding in Africa today.

The United States and other affluent countries, which use a disproportionate share of the world's raw materials, must learn to use natural resources far more efficiently, and the United States must move rapidly to stabilize its own population as an essential step in bringing the world's people and resources into equilibrium. (See Chapter 3 for other recommendations and further discussion of population growth.)

Energy Strategies

The best solution to U.S. and world energy problems relies predominantly on a variety of energy efficiency improvements in all sectors of the world economy. This strategy, sometimes called the soft energy path, affords significant economic, social, health, and environmental advantages over any other approach. By reducing dependence on other nations, this path enhances national security, whereas current U.S. policy undermines national security and harms the economy.

Efficiency improvements can make extraordinary differences in the energy requirement for industrial processes, lighting, transportation, and in buildings and homes. For example, the efficiency of lighting in the U.S. can be doubled, thereby saving more energy than is produced by all of the existing nuclear and hydro facilities combined. Automobiles achieving 60 to 90 miles per gallon are feasible today. Homes and buildings can be built to require no traditional heating or cooling. Recycling of aluminum saves 90 percent of the energy it takes to produce the same amount of aluminum from bauxite. Recycling of metals also reduces stockpiles of waste, causes less air and water pollution, and reduces the rapid depletion of strategic minerals.

These efficiency improvements are cheaper than any other source. Each quadrillion BTUs of energy saved through efficiency would cost at least $10 billion if produced from a traditional energy source (78 quadrillion BTUs of energy were consumed in 1984 in the United States).

Pursuit of the typical scenario outlined by the Department of Energy would involve increasingly serious demands on fossil fuel resources, and increased pollution with its attendant health risks. The high-energy-use scenarios forecast by the Department of Energy involve a 165 percent increase in sulfur dioxide emissions, which would increase acid rain and put larger amounts of carbon dioxide in the atmosphere, potentially threatening significant climate change.

The economical use of energy is well known to many industry and business leaders who, since the energy crisis of the mid-1970s, have found that introducing innovative processes to reduce energy consumption brings increased efficiency and higher profits. Several utilities have already recognized this fact and are planning to meet future energy growth almost entirely through non-traditional means. Instead of building costly large new coal or nuclear power plants, they are redirecting most of their investment funds into conservation and alternative sources. While planning to meet some future needs from conventional sources, they are managing energy loads more efficiently, practicing cogeneration (the simultaneous production of electricity and steam), and encouraging recycling.

As supplies of non-renewable resources dwindle in the future, competitive costs of providing them will increase and environmental damage from the development of new sources will grow. The development of renewable energy sources, including all forms of solar energy such as direct solar, biomass, and wind, can break the cycle of an increasingly limited fuel supply and its accompanying increase in costs.

The central goal should be to speed the shift to renewable energy use through such actions as removal of federal subsidies for energy production, full internalization of energy production costs, and mandatory efficiency standards for autos, appliances, and buildings. During the transition, steps must be taken to reduce the adverse environmental impacts caused by the use of conventional fuels. Methods of doing so include equipping fossil fuel plants with the latest pollution control technologies, substituting natural gas for coal and oil wherever practical and appropriate, and protecting human health and the land and water resources from the hazards of nuclear power—including the transportation, storage, and disposal of radioactive waste. (See Chapter 4 for other recommendations and further discussion of energy issues.)

Water Resources

Just as the best energy strategy for the nation is the pursuit of efficiency improvements in all sectors, so the best water resources strategy is to improve management of existing water projects and increase the efficiency of water use in the residential, agricultural, and industrial segments of the country.

This approach of improved efficiency has the potential to meet the nation's water needs at the least cost and with minimal environmental and social disruption. In contrast, the typical water development scenario of dams and channels favored by many politicians and well-entrenched water-use lobbies is a high cost path with many serious environmental and social impacts. The major challenge of the next 15 years will be to redirect institutions and redesign procedures to bring about the necessary shift to the efficiency path as smoothly and swiftly as possible.

Requiring users of water projects to pay the full costs of construction, operation, and maintenance, including external costs and interest charges that reflect long-term federal borrowing expense, will encourage a shift toward efficient use of water.

To safeguard groundwater sources from pollution and mining (pumping water at rates that exceed natural recharge), comprehensive state groundwater management laws are needed. These laws should provide for sustained-yield management, better mapping and monitoring of groundwater, a ban on mining of rechargeable aquifers, protection of groundwater quality against contamination, and incentives for industry to recycle toxic wastes into profitable new resources.

Demand for in-stream uses of water is growing rapidly as people use streams more intensively for fishing and other recreation. In many western states, however, water laws fail to recognize and protect these values. Action is needed on a state-by-state basis to recognize in-stream values and provide protective mechanisms, even though this will necessitate fundamental changes in state water laws.

With more than 50 percent of the nation's wetlands already destroyed, additional protection is needed to combat speculative drainage of wetlands for crops, subdivisions, or industry. A significant step toward protection of the remaining wetlands would be the repeal of federal tax laws that subsidize such activities. (See Chapter 5 for other recommendations and discussion of water resources.)

Toxics and Pollution Control

Despite much progress over the past two decades, when landmark pollution control legislation was enacted, most forms of pollution are not yet under control and many new problems exist. More than half of the U.S. population lives in areas where air pollutants still exceed health standards some of the time. The nation annually produces more than one ton per person of hazardous wastes. Eight years after Congress passed legislation to control the treatment, storage and disposal of hazardous waste, less than ten percent of the facilities currently handling wastes have been licensed. Five years after passage of the 1980 Superfund legislation to clean up dangerous, abandoned waste dumps, less than one percent of the known dumps have been cleaned up. Groundwater has been contaminated in areas throughout the nation, and tens of thousands of wells have been closed. The Environmental Protection Agency (EPA) has not adequately regulated pesticides.

More than 65,000 commercial chemicals identified by the National Academy of Sciences are currently being marketed, yet little or no data has been compiled on the potential many of them have to cause cancer, birth defects, or chronic diseases. Pesticides and toxic substances banned for use in the United States are allowed to be exported overseas or produced by U.S. companies in developing nations without full examination of the danger of accident or understanding of potential impacts on residents near manufacturing sites. Half of the water pollution that affects lakes and streams comes from non-point sources, particularly unregulated storm water runoff from city streets and runoff from agricultural lands. The amount of carbon dioxide and methane released into the atmosphere continues to increase rapidly, creating a threat of profound climate change in the future.

There is an urgent need to solve these problems and thus allow a complex industrial society to function and grow without endangering people and destroying or depleting the natural systems that sustain them. Activities that contaminate natural resources impose monetary and non-monetary costs upon all citizens, and the public has rejected the notion that pollution controls should be put in place only when monetary benefits exceed the dollar costs. The effects of pollution and benefits of control are not definable solely in monetary terms. Health, safety, and a liveable environment also should be seen as part of the national wealth. Environmental regulation can improve economic welfare and increase economic efficiency. An important goal of environmental regulation should be to minimize involuntary exposure to risk and to provide individuals with information about relative risks or alternative choices. Past experience has shown that it is better to take the side of safety.

Among high priorities for needed action by Congress are: passage of an effective safe drinking water law; extension and strengthening of Superfund and the Federal Insecticide, Fungicide and Rodenticide Act; amendment of the Clean Water Act to control non-point sources of surface water pollution; and enactment of acid rain legislation requiring a 50 percent reduction in sulfur dioxide emissions. In the new field of genetic engineering research and development, the federal government should adopt a policy of no release into the environment of gene engineered products without having a full understanding of potential effects. (See Chapter 6 for other recommendations and discussion of toxics and pollution control issues.)

Wild Living Resources

The planet today faces the immediate threat of a staggering loss of wild species, unequalled in history. The conservation of biological diversity—the immense variety and abundance of plant and animal life—and the maintenance or restoration of areas of natural habitat upon which species survival depends are of vital importance. This diversity of wild species forms the base from which future human needs may be met, ranging from genetic strains for improving agricultural products to new medicines.

Conserving biological diversity and maintaining or restoring natural plant and animal habitats are goals shared by people throughout the world. Since wild living organisms do not recognize national boundaries and since the areas of highest biological diversity, such as tropical forests which are critical to all of humanity, lie outside U.S. jurisdiction, extinction prevention and habitat protection must be addressed in international as well as domestic arenas.

Achieving these goals will require cooperative efforts among state, national, and international governments, and by universities, industry, and citizen groups. There are many examples of such cooperation. Two in North America are the reversal of the decline of the whooping crane population and the preservation of the grizzly bear in the U.S. northern Rocky Mountain area. On the global scene, progress toward saving the endangered and threatened whale species is of special significance.

State agencies dealing with wild living resources should be strengthened and provided with expanded revenues by means such as utilizing state income tax check-offs, or through fish and wildlife endowment funds that can help to prevent drastic fluctuation in agency funding. Federal and state programs should support conservation of wild plants and plant habitats, which have been sorely neglected. States should adopt or strengthen regulations and procedures to assess the potential harm to wild living resources and their habitats that could be wrought by development activities, and find alternative sites or methods of filling development needs when negative environmental impacts are detected.

Current standards delineating how much government actions may impinge on wild living resources must be assessed for their adequacy and enforced, and new standards set where none now exist. Federal and state governments should be encouraged to develop wild living resource conservation plans and assure that all major proposed governmental actions are consistent with those plans. Governments also should use relevant tax incentives, regulations, and subsidies to influence the actions of the private sector. The model provided by the recent coastal barrier islands legislation should be extended to discourage unsound development in wildlife habitat of special value.

Industrial nations should monitor and, where necessary, control their actions and those of multi-national corporations operating in developing nations and on the high seas to minimize their impact on biological diversity. (See Chapter 7 for other recommendations and discussion of wild living resource issues.)

Private Lands and Agriculture

Difficult environmental and resource problems surround privately held farmlands, range, forests, wetlands, and valuable natural areas in the United States. A variety of corrective measures are urgently needed for stemming the conversion of fragile lands to crop production, preventing the soil erosion and off-farm site damage that result from poor land management practices; protecting private forest land to enhance its watershed capabilities and maintain its ability to supply forage and provide fish and wildlife habitat; protecting private lands from degradation and pollution from mining; and protecting from development private lands that have natural and cultural values. The long-term viability of the land is closely tied to the resource base and its use.

Significant amounts of agricultural land are lost to development and urbanization each year despite fluctuating but generally increasing demand for export of U.S. farm products. Eroded soil laden with chemical nutrients and pesticides costs the nation hundreds of millions of dollars a year as it fills up reservoirs, adds to flood damage, clogs navigation facilities and canals, affects drinking water supplies, destroys aquatic wildlife, and diminishes recreational potential.

Curbing the irreversible loss of productive land will require a mix of federal, state, and local initiatives to remove incentives for conversion of prime farmland to non-agricultural uses, to improve state and local land-use planning and growth management, and to modify the federal programs that contribute to unnecessary or irreversible farmland conversion. Congress should enact a strong sodbuster policy that would penalize any farmer who plows up highly erodible land without taking soil prevention precautions. Similar provisions should be enacted to deny benefits to farmers who drain, fill, or otherwise convert wetlands to croplands.

Federal and state governments should strengthen laws to reduce non-point source pollution from private land and encourage new land management techniques that can safely and effectively reduce pollution and soil erosion.

Actions should be taken to improve the management and productivity of private forest lands, including amendment of the tax code to require those taking capital gains treatment to invest a significant proportion of the savings in reforestation.

A law providing for reclamation of abandoned mine sites should be enacted by Congress, modeled on existing coal mine reclamation laws.

To protect the important natural, cultural, and recreational resources not included in existing governmental land management systems, new preservation techniques should be adopted, such as establishing greenline parks through cooperation between the private sector and government at all levels. The greenline approach has been used effectively in New York's Adirondack Mountains and New Jersey's Pine Barrens. Another approach is that of establishing ecosystem management areas in places where economic use is intensive. This approach is being used in the cooperative local, state, and federal effort to save Chesapeake Bay.

Private national, state, and local land-saving conservation organizations, as well as government agencies, will need to continue and increase their activities that have resulted in acquisition of millions of acres of natural lands. It will also be necessary to multiply efforts to educate all citizens regarding the ethical use of land—acceptance of individual responsibility for the health of the land and a full understanding of how people are linked to and depend upon the land. (See Chapter 8 for other recommendations and discussion of private lands and agriculture.)

Protected Land Systems

The national park, wildlife refuge, wilderness preservation, wild and scenic river, marine sanctuary systems, and wildlands on the national forests protect some of the country's most important and outstanding natural resources and provide varied habitats necessary to support a rich and diverse wildlife heritage. At the same time they afford important outdoor recreational opportunities for the public and constitute a national heritage of scenic and cultural treasures. The existing federal sanctuaries, which have been established over the last century for the benefit of future generations, should be safeguarded from the increasing internal and external threats to their preservation. The most urgent need today is to add critical natural areas to existing systems before their unique values are lost to development or other factors, thus ensuring that suitable portions of all basic types of ecosystems receive appropriate protection.

The Land and Water Conservation Fund should be fully used to add new units to the national park and national wildlife refuge systems and to acquire private lands within national parks, as well as to complete existing refuge units. The protection of additional wetland habitat is especially important. Outstanding river segments on federal lands should be designated for the national wild and scenic rivers system with the goal of adding 70,000 miles of the 3.5 million river miles in the United States by the year 2000. State wild and scenic river programs should be established in states that lack them. Suitable areas should be added to the National Wilderness Preservation System to ensure that adequate portions of each of the nation's 232 basic ecosystems are protected. And all of the remaining roadless lands in the national park, national wildlife refuge, national forest, and Bureau of Land Management (BLM) systems should be reviewed for their suitability for addition to the National Wilderness Preservation System.

Data on the condition of natural resources in protected land systems is wholly inadequate for effective resource management. Federal agencies managing protected lands will need to prepare thorough inventories and conduct studies in order to complete adequate resource management plans. To combat threats to protected systems, legislation is needed establishing "zones of influence" to require that any federal activity or other activity on federal land adjacent to a protected land system unit be consistent with protection of the unit's resources. Congress should also provide an organic act that identifies the wildlife refuge system's purpose and specifies criteria for planning and management. (See Chapter 9 for other recommendations and discussion of protected land systems.)

Public Lands

In dealing with the nation's public lands, which comprise one-third of the land in the United States, more legal checks and balances are needed to prevent overexploitation of forest, range, and mineral resources. Planning is needed to ensure truly balanced multiple use of the lands so that timber production, mining, oil, and coal exploitation and grazing do not overshadow conservation values. Modern techniques of analysis should be applied to the management of public lands, and fees and sale prices of land should reflect fair market value, and should cover administrative costs. Timber from national forests should not be sold at a loss. Methods should be developed to protect areas of special natural value such as sensitive seabed and coastal zones, areas of critical environmental concern, and areas with old-growth timber. Between 15 and 25 percent of the remaining old-growth timber on each national forest should remain uncut to assure necessary biological diversity.

The government should undertake a coordinated program to rehabilitate the millions of acres of public rangelands that have been damaged by overgrazing, inappropriate mineral exploration and development, logging, or intensive recreational use. The growing national problem of desertification should be addressed. The economically unsound Mining Act of 1872 should be replaced with new legislation that provides for discretionary leasing, fair market royalties, environmental safeguards, rehabilitation of the land, and designation of areas that are unsuitable for mining.

Legislation is needed to establish standards for the prevention of adverse environmental effects on public lands from off-road vehicles. Congress should also develop a program of sustained funding to enable the Forest Service, by the end of the century, to purchase, or protect by other means such as land exchanges, additional private lands within the boundaries of every national forest with the goal of achieving Forest Service management over 50 to 75 percent of the forest area.

The National Oceanic and Atmospheric Administration should identify and map Outer Continental Shelf areas with special biological or environmental values, geologic hazard sites, and areas with commercial hard mineral, oil, or gas potential. The Secretary of the Interior should delete from development plans those areas with high biological values or geologic hazards and low commercial potential.

The Department of the Interior's coal leasing program should be reappraised by Congress. In 65 years of leasing, less than one billion tons out of the 18 billion tons of coal leased has been developed. The Department should not be allowed to hold new coal sales in any area until it can demonstrate the market need, and has removed all environmentally sensitive areas from potential leasing. (See Chapter 10 for other recommendations and discussion of public lands.)

Urban Environment

America's cities, home to more than 70 million people and centers of employment, shopping, and culture for millions who live in suburban areas, are facing difficult environmental and health problems into the next century.

Air quality is worse in urban areas than elsewhere, due to many factors such as concentration of emissions from motor vehicles and industry. Conversion by trucks and buses to diesel engines, with their dangerous particulate emissions, poses a growing health hazard that will require stricter standards and better inspection programs. Indoor air pollutants such as toxic chemicals used in cleaning agents and pesticides, gas from unvented indoor combustion, or substances such as asbestos and formaldehyde cause serious problems.

The growing risks of contamination of urban water supplies and the uncertainty surrounding the ability of many cities to satisfy future water demands require cooperative action from federal, state, and local regulatory agencies. The EPA needs to establish and enforce strict nationwide standards to control toxic contaminants in drinking water, and strengthen groundwater protections by tightly regulating the injection of industrial waste, the underground storage of toxic chemicals, and the application of pesticides in areas above aquifers. State and local governments should adopt stringent controls on land development in watershed areas to mitigate the impact of non-point pollution, and should adopt tax incentives for retrofitting inefficient water appliances, metering residential water use, and other conservation measures.

Garbage and other solid waste disposal problems will confront nearly every urban area over the next two decades. Unable to find space for landfills, and also recognizing the serious health and environmental problems landfills present, many municipal officials are turning to incineration of garbage. This raises potentially dangerous air quality problems. New technologies for solid waste disposal will need to be encouraged, and EPA should enforce stringent emissions limitations for garbage-burning incinerators.

The shift of population, jobs, and development from the inner cities to suburban areas that has occurred over the past 25 years has had major adverse environmental consequences such as loss of prime agricultural and recreational lands, threatened water supplies, and increased energy use. Congress should eliminate tax breaks, investments, grants, and loans for programs that encourage development of urban sprawl.

Urban sprawl also heightens the need for adequate public transportation. With greatly increased automobile and truck traffic predicted for urban areas over the next 15 years, the failure to resolve the public transit crisis in most cities is a major social and environmental problem. Public transit systems are inadequate, older ones are starved for funds, and newer systems remain incomplete. To help alleviate the crisis, Congress should increase the motor vehicle gasoline tax five cents a gallon. This could generate $5 billion a year for the federal transit fund earmarked to finance capital projects.

The few recreational facilities available to city dwellers are inadequate and many are deteriorating. Congress should allocate to the states higher levels of funding from the Land and Water Conservation Fund, to be used for urban open space and recreation. Congress should also create a national conservation corps and state and local governments should implement their own conservation corps. (See Chapter 11 for other recommendations and discussion of the urban environment.)

International Responsibilities

The health and availability of natural resources and the quality of the environment can no longer be treated as only of national concern. The destruction of the natural environment resulting from population expansion, industrial demands, unplanned and unchecked urbanization, and inappropriate development have effects that reach beyond the individual nations. Their impacts are felt in neighboring nations and across oceans and hemispheres. Polluted air or acid rain spreads far beyond national boundaries and water pollution affects shared river basins and oceans. Destruction of tropical forests, desertification of vast areas, and the potential exploitation of the Antarctic are now of universal concern. The economic distress, degradation of environmental quality, and displacement of peoples in many countries throughout the world and the ultimate disaster of nuclear war and an accompanying nuclear winter confront the world with a precarious future.

The security of the United States is increasingly dependent on the prosperity and stability of developing nations. Environmental stress plays a significant part in destabilizing governments. Worldwide environment, population, natural resource, and development problems are linked with the United States' self-interests, and challenge U.S. citizens to help in their resolution.

An essential requirement for dealing with long-term worldwide trends in environment, population, resources, and development is the establishment of a capacity within the Executive Office of the President to monitor and analyze these trends and bring such information to the attention of governmental policymakers. With such foresight capability, alternative decisions could be proposed that might change trends and prevent future crises.

Congress and relevant executive branches of the government should cooperate in taking steps to avoid global environmental catastrophes and improve environmental conditions. Increased funding should be made available for multilateral development institutions and the U.S. Agency for International Development. Such funding should be contingent on evidence that the proposed programs will focus significant attention on sustainability of resource use, adoption of environmentally sound projects, and the stabilization of human population. The development institutions and agencies should also abandon further funding for construction of large-scale projects that cause major social and environmental harm.

The United States should regularly pay its financial share for continuing programs of international agencies such as the United Nations Environment Programme, the United Nations Fund for Population Activities, the Food and Agriculture Organization, the Man and the Biosphere program, and the World Heritage Fund. Congress should enact legislation to regulate export of hazardous chemicals and pesticides and to promote the safe manufacturing operations of U.S. chemical firms abroad.

Congress and the Administration should ratify and adhere to the Law of the Sea Treaty, and the Administration should work to improve treaties concerned with protecting the oceans and the Antarctic. (See Chapter 12 for other recommendations and discussion of international issues.)

Conclusion

The key to the solution of most of the problems raised in this agenda for the future is public awareness of the issues and a recognition of the interconnections among population growth, natural resource availability, development, and environmental impacts. The general public and decision-makers need to understand the true costs of their own actions and those of government and the private sector and how to weigh the long-term, far-reaching benefits against the immediate, localized costs or risks.

Any consideration of the future must remain dynamic. Hence this agenda will be subjected to periodic review and revision as trends and circumstances require. The individual chapters on specific issues that follow are written with the intent of highlighting some of the environmental problems that are expected to command attention in the coming years while also discussing some of today's highest priorities, which will affect the future. In most cases the recommendations represent a consensus view. In the rare cases where there was disagreement, a majority position of the ten chief executive officers was adopted. Although the document does not represent the official positions of the organizations whose executives have authored it, we believe the product as a whole does represent a positive vision of the ways in which the American people can better protect their natural heritage while achieving a high quality of life and a healthy economy.

Carrying out the agenda will require the cooperation of individuals from all walks of life. The involvement and assistance of industry, labor, educators, scientists, lawyers, students, government workers, homemakers, and other elements of the society will be needed.

2

Nuclear Issues

The Consequences of a Nuclear War

In 1983 a group of scientists made public new findings on long-term climatic and biological impacts of nuclear war. These findings, released at the Conference on the World After Nuclear War and subsequently published in *Science,* described a range of ecological consequences that put nuclear war at the forefront of the environmental agenda. The scientists already knew that the immediate death and destruction from any nuclear exchange is so horrendous as to be unacceptable. But they found that in addition to the immediate effects, the explosion of even a relatively small number of high-yield nuclear weapons could plunge the entire earth into a catastrophe of stupendous proportions. Soot, smoke, dust, and other particulates and gases created by the nuclear blasts and resulting fires could form vast, dark clouds over most of the northern hemisphere, blocking out the sun. The outcome, beginning within two weeks and lasting for months, could be a man-made "nuclear winter." Darkness could persist around the clock, continental land temperatures could drop as low as minus 25 degrees celsius, surface waters could freeze to depths of up to six feet, and most plant and animal life could be destroyed. The earth's winds could eventually carry the nuclear pall around the globe, leaving no place to hide.

All of these long-term ecological effects would compound

the horror of massive human deaths and physical devastation from the nuclear blast, radiation, and fire, the disruption of social, political, and economic structures, and the collapse of normal medical services, communications, transportation, and food distribution.

The studies make clearer than ever that there can be no winners in a nuclear war. Practical civil defense against nuclear war has always been problematical; civil defense against a nuclear winter would be virtually impossible. The survivors of the initial blasts and radiation would face a cold, dark, depleted world in which survival would be extremely difficult. The eminent biologists participating in the nuclear winter studies have not ruled out the possibility of the extinction of the human species.

Since their release the nuclear winter findings have been subjected to intense scrutiny. A committee of the National Academy of Sciences gave a general endorsement to the nuclear winter theory in a 1984 study commissioned by the Department of Defense. And the Defense Department has also completed a congressionally-mandated study which acknowledges the scientific basis for the threat of nuclear winter. Detailed review is continuing in the United States, Soviet Union, Australia, and the Federal Republic of Germany. The results of a broad international effort under the auspices of the Scientific Committee on Problems of the Environment (SCOPE) of the International Council of Scientific Unions is scheduled to be released in 1985. These studies will address various uncertainties in the original research and are leading to refinements and modifications. Few, if any, reputable scientists believe that further research could eliminate completely the possibility of a nuclear winter following a nuclear exchange. Nevertheless, additional research is essential not only to give further scrutiny to the original findings but also to understand the manifold ramifications involved. While study on the various effects of nuclear weapons is accelerated, there must also be acknowledgement that further dangers exist which are not now known. By their very nature, these sorts of findings cannot be confirmed except by large-scale nuclear experimentation, which, of course, is unacceptable.

Even as scientific inquiry and examination proceed, the significance of the nuclear winter findings must be made more widely known and understood. Educational efforts at all levels should be expanded to make citizens and policymakers aware of the potential for unprecedented global catastrophe from the climatic and biological effects of any nuclear exchange. Citizen organizations can serve this function by undertaking several tasks: keeping themselves and the public informed about refinements and improvements to the original findings; incorporating the findings into their educational efforts about long-term threats to the global environment; identifying the policy implications of the findings; and bringing both the findings and their policy implications to the attention of decision-makers at all levels of government.

Throughout the Atomic Age, defense policy and nuclear strategy have been developed with only scant knowledge of the climatic and biological effects of nuclear war; even the existing knowledge of effects was largely disregarded by policymakers. Today, scientific understanding of nuclear war's consequences has increased dramatically, but traditional military approaches persist. Planners still talk of "limited" nuclear wars, of one side "prevailing" in a nuclear confrontation, and of civil defense assuring the "survival" of society. There has been no indication that the threat of global extinction has changed the way policymakers think about nuclear weapons and war. Einstein's dictum still holds after almost 40 years: "The unleashed power of the atom has changed everything save our modes of thinking, and thus we drift toward unparalleled catastrophe." It is therefore essential that education about nuclear winter focus on the necessity of changing policy and strategy to address the problem. The need to inject consideration of environmental consequences into nuclear weapons policy debates has never been greater.

In view of the scientific findings as to the dire consequences on the life support system of the planet, and the substantial probability that any use of nuclear weapons could escalate into conditions that could trigger nuclear winter, the inescapable conclusion is that nuclear weapons must never again be used. As a first step toward assuring that they will not be, the superpowers should vigorously pursue a mutual and verifiable moratorium on the testing, production, and deployment of nuclear weapons.

Dangers of Nuclear Arms in Time of Peace

The acute and far-reaching devastation of nuclear war and the costly diversion of resources toward preparation for waging nuclear war demand increased efforts to limit development and deployment of nuclear weapons. However, the threat to environmental health and human welfare presented by the current nuclear arms race is neither potential nor contingent; its damage is being done today. Nuclear weapons production and testing activities directly degrade the environment and continue to pose an immediate health and safety danger to employees and the general public through toxic and radioactive contamination of air, water, and food. These rapidly accelerating pollution problems created by weapons production are significant health and environmental dangers that have gone largely unconsidered.

Several U.S. nuclear weapons facilities have the potential for causing catastrophic radioactive contamination and loss of life from accidents. A major acceleration of nuclear weapons production and testing requires a tremendous expansion of these facilities. The risk is that such an expansion would amount to the extension of the dangerous facilities already in place, thereby increasing the severe pollution problems and the further danger of catastrophic accident.

The Department of Energy (DOE) owns the entire complex of U.S. nuclear warhead design, production, and testing facilities. DOE's nuclear weapons program is responsible for more than 100 million gallons of long-lived radioactive wastes—over 90 percent of the total U.S. volume—and there is no safe place to store them. Wastes from weapons manufacturing, combined with highly-toxic organic solvents, mercury, and polychlorinated biphenals (PCBs), are produced and stored near population centers where they pose a continuing threat to large numbers of people. In Aiken, South Carolina, for instance, wastes from the Savannah River Plant have already entered regional water supplies. The plant has dumped an estimated ten tons of mercury in burial pits at the facility. These pits and high-level waste tanks sit atop a series of underground aquifers that provide a major drinking water supply for four states. Groundwater at the site now contains mercury, plutonium, tritium, and strontium-90 in excess of EPA drinking water standards, and a deep freshwater aquifer has been contaminated with organic solvents from the plant.

These threats are not theoretical. Citizens must recognize the potential health costs and threats to human life involved in development of nuclear weapons systems. Surveys reveal abnormally high cancer incidence and mortality rates among the 600,000 people who have worked in weapons facilities since the 1940s and among the quarter-million military personnel who took part in atmospheric nuclear weapons tests. The surveys show that those people working in or living near nuclear weapons facilities are at greater risk than those in commercial nuclear power and chemical industries. Consequently the natural and human environment in surrounding communities is also at greater risk.

The controversial health and environmental legacy of commercial nuclear power has given impetus to the efforts of those people working to curtail warhead material production and testing. Environmental lawsuits have forced the release of information indicating that these government facilities are among the most serious violators of toxic waste laws. Under the National Nuclear Waste Policy Act, citizens and state officials have fought DOE decisions to relax nuclear waste management practices and avoid greater Nuclear Regulatory Commission oversight of its waste program. Citizens in regions that host DOE weapons facilities, and those who live along nuclear transportation routes also are pressuring DOE to clean up and safely dispose of radioactive and toxic wastes, to meet tougher worker health and safety standards, and to provide compensation for radiation injuries.

Historically, direct threats to health have caused Americans to become involved in nuclear arms control. The cessation of atmospheric nuclear weapons testing in 1963 was largely due to citizen concern over widespread radioactive contamination of the biosphere from weapons testing fallout. A similar concern was influential in the ratification of the Anti-Ballistic Missile Treaty. The long-term biological effects of the production and use of nuclear weapons now raises a legitimate need for the people in nations that have nuclear capabilities to question not only when and if nuclear weapons are used, but also the danger to human health and the environment from weapons production.

In the effort to protect themselves from the hazards of nuclear weapons production, concerned citizens are seeking to force a more complete accounting of all environmental, as well as financial, costs of the government's program. Because of the high costs associated with meeting state-of-the-art health and safety standards, Congress has, since 1982, delayed providing funds for building a new nuclear weapons production reactor to replace aging facilities. Many members of Congress are also concerned that providing funds for the new production reactor would result in less funding being available for the necessary cleanup of military radioactive wastes.

If the superpowers were to freeze the arms race, no new facilities would be needed. The current U.S. nuclear arsenal is reported to contain 26,000 warheads representing an explosive yield of 5,000 to 8,000 megatons. Scientists estimate that the United States has amassed about 100 metric tons of plutonium-239 and about 500 to 700 metric tons of highly enriched uranium, more than enough warhead materials to meet national security needs. The connections between protecting the environment and halting the nuclear arms race are clear and compelling.

Any agreement to limit nuclear weapons systems would be a temporary measure in the absence of limits on the production of nuclear explosives. A race between the superpowers to amass more nuclear explosives poses serious health and environmental problems. Unfortunately, countries with nuclear weapons have already incurred serious public health abuses, although all of these nations deny that their nuclear activities have subjected thousands of people to dangerous radiation exposures.

Recommendations

Mutual Verifiable Moratorium

In view of the scientific findings regarding nuclear winter, and the high probability that any use of nuclear weapons could escalate, the inescapable fact is that nuclear weapons must never be used. The proliferation of nuclear weapons multiplies the hazards.

- Citizens, working through their elected representatives, should oppose this nuclear buildup, especially through the funding process. Congress should call for a mutual and verifiable moratorium, to be negotiated by the United States, the Soviet Union, and other nuclear nations, on the production, testing, and deployment of nuclear weapons; and should support non-proliferation policies that will limit the spread of nuclear weapons and prevent the distribution of hazardous materials around the world.

Policy Implications of Nuclear Winter

Recent research on the climatic and biological effects of nuclear weapons adds greatly to human understanding of the nuclear threat and has important policy implications for nuclear strategy and arms control.

- Public interest organizations should expand citizen education efforts, emphasizing the policy implications of the nuclear winter findings. Education efforts should present nuclear war as the the ultimate environmental threat now confronting the world, reaffirm that the nuclear arms race is incompatible with human survival, and integrate health and environmental pollution issues more directly into the nuclear arms debate.

Nuclear winter findings merit further scientific study, but research cannot substitute for thorough policy re-evaluation and adjustment.

- The President, Defense Department, State Department, and Arms Control and Disarmament Agency should immediately re-evaluate nuclear weapons, arms control, and civil defense policies and programs in light of the nuclear winter findings. This re-evaluation should be the subject of full public review and debate.

Nothing should preclude consideration of the consequences and the environmental impacts, including worst-case scenarios, for all Department of Defense and Department of Energy projects involving nuclear weapons and their components.

- The Federal Government should immediately re-evaluate nuclear weapons production policies with regard to their effect on health and the environment. A similar proposal should be made to the Soviet Union. All branches of government should comply fully with all existing environmental laws and regulations, and all agencies should enforce those laws fully as they apply to nuclear weapons systems, their production, and testing.

Weapons Production Safety and Health

Government-operated nuclear weapons production and testing facilities have lower health and safety standards than commercial industries. The Department of Energy has continuously ignored public health protection principles and has repeatedly violated toxic waste laws.

- Congress should strengthen health and safety standards at nuclear production and assembly facilities by transferring oversight for health-related decisions from DOE to the National Institutes of Health, the Environmental Protection Agency, the Nuclear Regulatory Commission, and state governments. DOE should meet industry pollution standards.

3

Human Population Growth

In the past 10,000 years, human populations have reached or exceeded the carrying capacity of their local or regional environment many times, and human societies have sometimes paid the price of a population collapse. But now, in just the past few decades, the human species has begun to strain the limits of the global biological systems that support all life—the oceans, grasslands, croplands, wetlands, and forests. Human beings are consuming the earth's productive resource base at the same time that our growing numbers require more resources. We are depleting our biological capital.

There are now 4.8 billion human beings. It took Homo sapiens a million years to reach a population of one billion (in 1830); it is now taking only 13 years to add the fifth billion—an increase comparable to the current population of China. At the present rate of growth, there will be more than six billion people on the earth by the end of the century.

The most rapid growth is occurring in the already-populous Third World in Asia, Africa, and Latin America. There some 800 million human beings live in conditions that the World Bank has described as "absolute poverty . . . a condition of life degraded by disease, illiteracy, malnutrition, and squalor. . . ."

Almost half of the world's people live in the rural areas of developing countries. Caught in a daily struggle for enough food and fuel to stay alive, they strip the land of trees and bushes for firewood. They clear steep hillsides for farming, only to have the soil washed away by rains. Their goats and cattle overgraze grassy drylands, which then become deserts. They overfish and overhunt local wildlife.

Because the land cannot support additional family members, many rural people are forced to migrate to crowded cities where they find shelter in slums and shanty towns. The population of many Third World cities is now doubling every 10 years or less. In many countries, population growth is outstripping economic growth, causing a decline in per capita income.

Beyond Biological Limits

Until world population reached three billion in 1960, the yields of the basic biological systems expanded more rapidly than population. At that point, however, the margin began to narrow. Population growth outstripped forest production after 1964. Since 1970, the fish catch per person has fallen by 13 percent. As world population passed four billion, grasslands production of beef, mutton, and wool began to fall behind population growth. Overfishing, overgrazing, and overcutting have become widespread. As demand exceeds the sustainable yield of biological systems, the human species is beginning to consume the productive resource base itself.

In Kenya, at present birth rates, the human population is doubling every 14 years. Kenya's superb wildlife resources are being extinguished because of poaching and habitat loss as the human population expands so rapidly.

A report from the U.S. Embassy in Indonesia indicates that soil erosion is bringing on an "ecological emergency" in Java, laying waste to the land much faster than present reclamation programs can restore it.

In Ethiopia, an environmental nightmare is unfolding—the result of millions of Ethiopians struggling for survival, attempting to cultivate already eroded land and thus eroding it further, cutting down the trees for cooking and heating, and leaving the country denuded. Over one billion tons of topsoil washes from Ethiopia's highlands each year.

In Africa, the Middle East, Afghanistan, and northwestern India, the deserts are expanding as human and livestock populations increase. Although its southward spread gets more attention, the Sahara is also extending northward toward the Mediterranean, overrunning what was once the granary of the Roman Empire.

Forage specialists estimate that the rangelands of northern Iraq can safely sustain only 250,000 sheep without degradation—a far cry from the million or so sheep currently eating away this resource base. Likewise, Syria's ranges are carrying three times the number of grazing animals they can support on a sustainable basis.

With an estimated 40 percent of the world's population using wood as its primary fuel, the drain on the world's forests is immense. In 1950, roughly 25 percent of the earth's land surface was covered by trees; by 1980, less than 20 percent had tree cover. Along with firewood collecting, the leading cause of deforestation is the expansion of crop and livestock production. In Central America and Brazil, forest land is being cleared for grazing, largely to produce beef that is exported to the United States. The cost of this conversion is high, particularly since tropical soils may not sustain grass production for long.

At least two-thirds of all species of plants and animals on Earth have their habitat in the tropics. Through the loss of tropical forests, species are becoming extinct at a rate of hundreds, perhaps even thousands, each year, and the extinction rate is likely to accelerate as human population grows. Yet the human species depends increasingly on these life forms for agriculture, medicine, energy, and pest control.

Impact on the United States

Global population growth is now affecting the United States in many ways, and its impact on the lives of our children and grandchildren could be far greater.

South of our border, the burgeoning populations of Mexico and Central America are causing an unprecedented surge of migration, legal and illegal, into the United States. Each year, larger numbers of Haitians, Guatemalans, Salvadorans, and other Central Americans reach working age. In societies already plagued by widespread poverty and economic inequality, these expanding legions of unemployed youths are the raw material for future instability in their own countries. For many of them, emigration to the United States is an escape valve.

The U.S. population, now about 237 million, grew by nearly 2.5 million during 1983. Much of this annual increase was due to immigration. At its present growth rate of about one percent annually, the United States is adding another Los Angeles to its population every year, a new California every decade.

The U.S. also feels the effects of the tropical forest loss throughout the world, for the resulting decline in the global wood supply puts pressures on U.S. forests. In addition, the wholesale cutting of tropical forests could bring about serious future climatic changes.

The countries of the Middle East had a multitude of problems in 1950 when there were 54 million people trying to solve their differences. There are now 134 million, and rapid population growth keeps fanning the religious, ethnic, and political turmoil that threatens international access to the world's largest oil reserve. A nagging danger for the United States and the rest of the world is that a future Middle East military conflict involving the superpowers could escalate into World War III and the ultimate human and environmental catastrophe.

Population pressures on the United States—from within, through national population growth, and from outside, through global demand for U.S. food—are being felt in various ways. The Los Angeles basin, the southwestern Sun Belt, southern Florida, and the Chesapeake Bay region are areas where rapid population influx has overtaxed the natural carrying capacity of the land. Other signs of population pressure, aggravated by resource mismanagement, may be seen in the depletion of the Ogallala aquifer underlying the southern plains states, the logging of remnant primeval forests in the Pacific Northwest, and a host of negative effects on other components of Earth's ecosystems that are now endangered primarily because of expanding human activities.

In all of the above examples, better conservation practices would help to solve or alleviate the problems for the time being. But resource depletion and environmental degradation are merely symptoms of the basic problem—the inexorable pressure being placed on the natural environment by a growing human population.

Unlike most countries, where the increasing demand for food is internally generated, the stresses on the U.S. soils come from mounting food deficits worldwide. The U.S. Department of Agriculture reported in 1981 that the inherent productivity of 34 percent of U.S. cropland is now falling because of the excessive loss of topsoil caused by overly intensive farming.

Meanwhile, population pressures within this country result in the loss of large amounts of cropland every year. While shopping centers, highways, reservoirs, and subdivisions infringe on the more desirable farmland, fragile hillsides and highly erodible prairies are increasingly brought under the plow.

Global Progress

Population growth can be controlled, and the rate of increase is already being slowed in some nations around the world.

Countries that have markedly reduced birth rates include China, South Korea, and Taiwan in eastern Asia, along with the city states of Hong Kong and Singapore. In the Caribbean, Barbados and Cuba have succeeded in lowering birth rates. Indonesia, Thailand, Colombia, and Costa Rica are making progress.

The countries that have achieved rapid national fertility declines represent a wide variety of cultures. The common denominators are a committed leadership and locally implemented family planning programs.

There is some cause for optimism. Attitudes of leadership in the developing countries have changed. A decade ago, many in the Third World were suspicious or hostile towards family planning for ideological, nationalistic, or religious reasons. Today, most leaders recognize that rapid population growth impedes social and economic progress. As a result, at least 47 developing countries have adopted population programs that include the provision of family planning services. These countries account for most of the people who live in the Third World.

But there are no grounds for complacency. Although the population growth rate has shown a slight decline, more people were added to the world in 1984 than in any other year in history. The delivery of family planning services is still woefully inadequate in most developing countries, particularly in rural areas. This means continued high rural population growth, environmental deterioration, and rural-to-urban migration. The end result is increased human misery and political unrest.

An estimated 600 million people in the developing world desire to limit the size and determine the spacing of their families. But they lack access to family planning services. As essential as these services are, however, they are not in themselves sufficient. The desired family size in many countries is still four or five children. Although that is a lower number than just a few years ago, that many children would cause a population gain that would steadily reduce living standards. Reducing fertility to the level needed for sustainable human progress calls for public education concerning the relationship between population and resources, respect for the traditions of indigenous peoples, and an understanding of the economic consequences parents and their children will face if the current demographic pattern continues.

Recommendations

U.S. Population Policy

The United Nations has projected a leveling off of world population at just over 10 billion, more than twice today's global population. If greater resources were dedicated to family planning efforts now, and if, as a consequence, a global average of a two-child family could be reached by the year 2000, world population would stabilize at about eight billion people by the middle of the next century. Our goals for slowing population growth should be consistent not only with a sustainable society but also with continuing improvements in the human condition.

- **The Administration should establish formal population policies, including goals for the stabilization of population at a level that will permit sustainable management of resources and a reasonably high quality of life for all people.**
- **To advance the goal of zero population growth, population organizations and other public interest groups should provide information through their publications, enlist knowledgeable speakers at organization functions, increase grass-roots and national legislative lobbying, work with the news media to publicize the need for and steps toward population stabilization, and include the implications of population growth in all environmental education programs.**

Aid to Developing Countries

International development assistance in general, and support for family planning programs in particular, has not kept pace with the need. This is especially true of the assistance provided by the United States, once the world leader in furthering population stabilization worldwide. For the past two decades, U.S. development assistance has steadily declined, both in dollars and as a share of the GNP. The greatest barrier to expansion of family planning services in the developing countries is lack of funds, and U.S. assistance should be increased.

- Congress and the Executive Branch should support the work of the United Nations Fund for Population Activities with adequate appropriations.
- U.S. non-government organizations and their affiliates should work with their counterparts in other countries to increase funding for population stabilization programs.

Development Agencies

Too often projects funded by the U.S. Agency for International Development, the World Bank, and other international assistance organizations have been undertaken without adequate concern for their impact on the environment or the indigenous peoples affected, the long-term sustainability, of the projects, or their effect on population patterns.

- The U.S. Agency for International Development should incorporate family planning in all its economic assistance programs for individual countries.
- The World Bank, the Inter-American Development Bank, the Asian Development Bank, and other funding institutions should give increased priority to population stabilization and environmental factors as part of their economic assistance.

4

Energy Strategies

Developing a strategy for meeting the country's energy needs is an exciting challenge. There is a quiet revolution beginning in homes, communities, and industries. People are finding out that they can use less energy in their homes and offices, save thousands of dollars, and not sacrifice comfort. Industries are realizing that investments in more efficient technologies and processes can save energy and improve corporate profits. Utilities are adopting load management strategies and beginning to invest in small-scale renewable energy sources as an alternative to building new coal and nuclear plants. It is possible to reduce oil imports, and the use of coal and nuclear power, and still not need a multi-billion-dollar synthetic fuels industry.

However, the Department of Energy (DOE) is planning for a very different energy future. DOE's plan suggests that the way to reduce the problems of global warming and acid rain associated with burning of fossil fuels is to build more nuclear plants; the way to become independent from foreign oil is to create a synthetic fuels industry; the way to have a strong economy is to produce and consume more energy from all sources. According to DOE projections, by the end of the century the United States will be importing more oil, burning more coal, using more nuclear power, and paying billions of dollars for synthetic fuels. It is a vision that is likely to cause environmental destruction, economic disaster, and possibly even push the nation to the brink of war over Middle East oil.

The soft energy path outlined in this chapter would bring about a cleaner environment, fewer international tensions, and a stronger economy. The best energy strategy is to increase greatly the productivity of the energy currently used and to shift to a future based on renewable energy sources.

For such a vision to become a reality, citizens need to take control of their energy future and become involved in energy planning in their neighborhoods, and at local, state, and federal government levels. In many places this is already happening, and the progress is substantial. But in the decades to come the initial successes can be duplicated, new strategies created, and emerging opportunities seized.

Implications of U.S. Energy Use

Energy is something few people consciously think about, yet it is used every day to move people from one place to another, to fuel industries, heat and light buildings, and operate appliances. When people think about energy costs, they usually think in terms of their own pocketbooks—how much it costs to fill the car with gas or pay the monthly utility bill. Yet the more significant costs are those related to the type of energy used and the way it is produced. Some sources of energy damage the environment, others burden the economy, and still others dangerously increase international tensions. Each of the sources of energy on which the United States depends has specific social, economic, and environmental costs. To develop an energy policy with the lowest possible costs, it is important to recognize the consequences of energy choices.

The international implications of U.S. energy policy are enormous. The U.S. has warned that it would go to war to "protect" foreign oil supplies or the supplies of American allies. Continued dependence on a handful of unstable nations in volatile regions of the world could trigger a major war. While this would be the ultimate tragic impact of present energy policies, there are many other very significant social and international consequences.

Although all consumers feel the financial impact of energy use, the types of energy chosen and the amounts used have far-reaching impacts on all parts of the economy. In addition, many of the costs of the energy consumed are not included in the price paid by consumers.

A number of the most pressing environmental issues of the past decade—from acid rain and radioactive waste to the destruction of wilderness areas—have been the direct result of U.S. energy policies. Not only will these problems persist in the coming decades, but serious new environmental problems will arise if the nation continues to rely on traditional fuel sources.

Building a Sustainable Energy Future

The development of a sustainable energy future would be based on the following principles:

- more efficient use of existing energy supplies and resources;
- the internalization of the full costs of energy production, including environmental impacts and health effects on workers and the public;
- a shift to renewable sources for meeting future energy needs;
- development of small-scale, decentralized energy-producing facilities, with increased citizen and local control.

Implementing this vision is an enormous challenge. Achieving such goals will require a significant commitment of resources, in both time and money, but this strategy is far less costly than DOE's scenario. The first step in building a sustainable energy future is to change the way Americans think about energy. Instead of considering it something people need to consume in ever-increasing quantities, it should be thought of in terms of the services it provides. No one wants energy for its own sake; energy is needed to provide mobility, comfort, and conveniences, and for processing goods and providing services. Energy requirements should be determined by looking first at the service to be performed and then choosing the most economical and appropriate way to accomplish the task.

Energy Efficiency

By the end of the century, energy efficiency can become the most important and the cheapest source of "new" energy. In addition, it provides a safer and more equitable way to meet U.S. energy needs than does new production.

In 1983, the American economy used nearly 25 percent less energy to produce each dollar of product than it did in 1973. Yet for many Americans, the myth that energy conservation means sacrificing creature comforts has not been totally dispelled. To make the most of the opportunities for improvements in energy efficiency, it is essential to convey to friends, neighbors, and elected officials the true value and benefits of energy conservation. Energy conservation means reducing waste and increasing productivity. It means substituting knowledge and technology for fuel. Futhermore, energy efficiency is cheaper than any other source. Each quadrillion BTUs of energy saved through efficiency would cost at least $10 billion if produced from a traditional energy source (78 quadrillion BTUs were consumed in 1984 in the United States).

Opportunities are abundant for improving efficiency in the three major energy-consuming sectors—transportation, buildings, and industry.

Transportation

Nearly one-third of U.S. energy is used to move people and things from one place to another. To meet transportation needs, the nation burns the equivalent of 6.5 million barrels of oil per day as gasoline. By substituting knowledge and technology for fuel it is possible to make dramatic improvements in the efficiency of vehicles and reduce the need for more fuel.

Automobiles, the largest single source of fuel consumption, represent the greatest potential for savings. Experts estimate that, without any major technological breakthroughs, a new car average of 60 miles per gallon is achievable by 1995. But without additional fuel economy standards, the United States is unlikely to move beyond an average of 25 miles per gallon.

Buildings

About one-third of U.S. energy is used in buildings—for heating and cooling the air, heating water, providing light, and operating major appliances. Cost-effective opportunities for increasing energy efficiency in residential and commercial buildings are abundant. Efficiency improvements range from very low-cost measures such as basic caulking, weatherstripping, and the adjusting of furnaces and the thermostats on water heaters to the installation of highly sophisticated computerized energy management systems.

Efficiency improvements in buildings have lagged behind other sectors primarily because of market imperfections. Since most new houses and commercial buildings are built by contractors who want to minimize initial expenses, cost-effective investments in efficient appliances and heating and lighting systems are often overlooked. Incentives for improvements in existing buildings are also very weak. More than one-third of the nation's housing is occupied by renters who usually are responsible for paying the utility bills, leaving landlords with no incentive to invest in weatherization or other basic efficiency improvements.

In some places community groups are overcoming these barriers by working cooperatively with local businesses, banks, and contractors to reduce energy consumption.

Another innovative approach to cutting energy waste in rental and low-income housing is the use of Energy Conservation Companies, or ECCOs. An ECCO provides up-front capital for weatherization and basic efficiency improvements under an arrangement whereby future energy savings are shared by the ECCO and the building owner. ECCOs have been successful in Europe for years and are just beginning to become popular in the United States.

Financial institutions, particularly mortgage lenders, could play a critical role in stimulating energy efficiency. Favorable financing packages for energy-efficient homes and buildings would provide builders and contractors with a considerable incentive to pay closer attention to efficiency improvements.

As the capital barriers and market imperfection are overcome, the total energy that could be saved in buildings is astounding. It has been estimated that improved appliance efficiency alone could eliminate the need for between 40 and 100 large power plants by the end of the century. Some experts estimate that cost-effective measures could reduce total energy consumption in buildings by as much as 30 percent over the next two decades, despite a 15 to 20 percent increase in building stock.

Industry

US. industries—factories, mines, farms, and construction—consume more than one-third of the country's energy. Over the past decade, industrial energy savings have already exceeded many expectations, but this is just the beginning. Until recently, industrial energy costs were usually included under the category of general overhead. The traditional way that industry executives looked at energy consumption changed when energy costs began increasing at a much faster rate than the other costs of doing business. As a result, industry executives have begun to realize that investing in energy efficiency improvements can be one of the most cost-effective ways to improve their company's bottom line.

The opportunities for reducing energy consumption in industry are enormous. Many companies are changing their output mix, shifting to less-energy-intensive products. Others are changing their production techniques, shifting from batch processing to continuous processing. Something as simple as shifting to more efficient lighting systems can significantly reduce energy use. Flourescent lights are three times as efficient as traditional incandescent lights; metal halide lamps can be nine times as efficient as incandescent lights, and high-pressure sodium lamps can be as much as ten times as efficient. More efficient lighting could save 35 percent more energy than all the nuclear plants or hydrodams in the U.S. now produce.

As a result of increased awareness of the potential of efficiency, energy service companies have become a rapidly growing new industry. Some of these companies develop new products and processes for improving energy efficiency. Others provide sophisticated computerized energy management systems, which reduce energy consumption in office and industrial heating, cooling, lighting, and other energy-intensive activities.

Industrial cogeneration, the simultaneous production of electricity and useful process steam, is one of the most promising technology improvements. Cogenerated electricity can be used at the industrial site, sold to a neighboring industry, or sold to a utility for redistribution.

Recycling of materials is another very important way to reduce industrial energy consumption. One fourth of the nation's energy is used to extract and process raw materials. When metal, glass, paper, and rubber are recycled, the energy that would be used to mine and process new raw materials is saved.

The potential energy savings from aggressive recycling programs are significant. Recycling one ton of steel uses only 14 percent of the energy needed to produce a ton of steel from raw materials. Recycling aluminum saves 95 percent of the energy it takes to produce the same amount of aluminum from bauxite.

In addition to saving energy, recycling is one of the most effective ways to reduce the nation's stockpile of toxic wastes and decrease air and water pollution. National security is another reason to recycle materials. As reserves of strategic minerals dwindle, the U.S. is becoming increasingly dependent on foreign countries for key minerals. By recycling these resources, the U.S. can reduce the pressures to extract minerals from environmentally sensitive areas and at the same time reduce the possibility of becoming involved in military struggles over strategic minerals.

Shifting to Renewables

The bulk of current energy supply comes from finite sources—oil, coal, natural gas, uranium. As supplies of these non-renewable resources dwindle, costs will unavoidably increase and social tensions between competitors for the fuel will grow. Environmental damage will become a growing problem as energy companies search for new supplies of fossil fuels in environmentally sensitive areas.

Renewable energy sources, which include all forms of solar energy such as biomass, wind, and direct solar, break the cycle of a limited fuel supply and its accompanying costs. Although renewable resources should be able to meet all of the nation's energy needs in the future, its development should be carefully managed to prevent troubling environmental problems.

Direct solar. The use of both active and passive solar energy systems in meeting space and water heating needs is already displacing conventional energy sources in many homes and commercial buildings. Industrial applications of solar technology in process heat is also increasing in popularity. Photovoltaic systems, which convert sunlight into direct electric current, are expected to become economically competitive with other sources of electricty in the 1990s. Small-scale photovoltaic cogeneration systems are already competitive for some uses.

Energy from the sun is the world's most abundant and only truly inexhaustible fuel source, but it would be a mistake to assume that it is totally free or environmentally benign. Direct and active solar systems depend to a certain extent on the production of non-renewable resources such as copper, and therefore the hazards associated with extraction and processing of these resources must be carefully managed as we expand the use of solar energy technology.

Biomass. The largest supply of solar energy in the near term will come from biomass, which is the use of crops and other vegetation to produce fuel. In fact, biomass already supplies about three percent of the country's energy needs. The use of biomass for steam-electric generation and industrial process steam generation could make use of significant existing municipal and industrial wastes and forestry and crop residues. The development of ethanol and methanol could become important in the transportation and industrial sectors. Although sources of biomass are abundant, the environmental impacts of biomass must be carefully considered to avoid serious air pollution, agricultural, and land-use problems.

Wind. Wind power is an unconventional energy source that is already an important part of some utilities' energy mix. Wind power is being produced in dispersed locations and with present small turbines at one-fourth to one-half the cost of electricity from new nuclear reactors. Because of their small scale and the short lead-time needed to build them, wind-powered generators are an attractive investment for many utilities.

Implementing a New Energy Vision

The fundamental problem in reaching the new energy vision will be to redirect massive amounts of investment capital into efficiency improvements and renewable energy sources. While this shift in investment capital will create new economic opportunities, it represents a threat to many very powerful political and economic interests. Developing strategies to accomplish this shift is an enormous challenge. The immediate goals include shifting from the most environmentally damaging energy sources, internalizing the full costs of each energy source, redefining the role of utilities, and directing government efforts toward sustainable energy policies.

Shifting Away from Environmentally Damaging Sources. The shift to renewable energy sources will not happen overnight, nor can it be completed within the next decade. The length of the transition will depend on the ability to implement energy efficency improvements and the speed with which renewable technologies replace conventional energy sources.

During the transition, reliance on conventional fuel sources will continue. Because of the severity of the environmental problems associated with these fuel sources, steps will need to be taken to lessen their adverse environmental impacts. Fossil fuel plants should be retrofitted with the state-of-the-art pollution control technologies. Natural gas, the cleanest of the fossil fuels, should be substituted for coal and oil wherever it is practical and appropriate. To the extent that nuclear power continues to be used, local communities should be protected from the hazards posed in all phases of the nuclear fuel cycle, from the mining and milling of uranium to the transportation, storage, and disposal of radioactive waste.

In areas where hydropower is going to be pursued as a

source of energy, it is better to retrofit existing dams with generators than to build new hydrodams. The vast majority of the 60,000 existing dams in the United States produce no power. The cumulative impacts of multiple energy projects, especially hydro, within the same watershed is one of the newly-emerging environmental problems that must be closely monitored and minimized.

In making the transition from conventional energy sources care must be taken to avoid moving toward new sources that present even greater problems. The current federal synthetic fuels commercialization program offers a good example. Synthetic fuels technologies present a multitude of environmental, technical, and economic uncertainties. Synfuels commercialization will generate huge land disturbances, pose significant threats to ground water supplies, and produce numerous toxic substances that are not adequately regulated by current law. Projects that have applied for federal assistance have proposed such damaging activities as the strip mining of peat from more than 100,000 acres of coastal wetlands and the disposal of thousands of tons of spent shale in a canyon with a creek that leads into the Colorado River. Moreover, billions of dollars in federal subsidies offered for synfuels commercialization create an artificial incentive that attracts industry into a market it would otherwise avoid. These programs, plagued with uncertainties, will siphon off a disproportionate share of potential energy investments for unproductive technologies.

Internalization of Energy Costs. Full internalization of all of the costs of each energy source is a critical element for developing a rational energy policy. The costs of scrubbers and other pollution control technologies need to be fully internalized in the price of fossil fuels. Similarly, the costs of the health effects from each energy source should be reflected in the price. The full costs of the nuclear fuel cycle, including decommissioning nuclear plants, disposal of wastes, and full insurance of accidents, are still largely unknown. An accurate assessment of many of these costs will be difficult to determine, and full internalization is likely to take years; but market forces will gradually shift the flow of investment capital toward those sources that meet energy needs most economically.

Redefining the Role of Utilities. Utilities in this country are in a period of transition; several are even at the brink of bankruptcy. The problems are largely caused by reliance on conventional wisdom. The solution to the current utility crisis is to begin looking at "unconventional" ways of doing business.

Until recently, utilities have been rewarded for building "bigger and better" central-station power facilities. In recent years an unanticipated decline in the growth of electric demand, combined with unprecedented cost overruns and construction delays at large new power plants, has forced many utilities into a financial crisis. As consumer rates are increased to pay for new plants, demand decreases further and the markets for new power disappear.

A few utilities are beginning to redefine their roles from providers of electricity to suppliers of a wide range of energy services. State public utility commissions should encourage this option for all utilities because providing reliable energy services instead of simply selling kilowatt hours is environmentally sound.

In California, two of the oldest and largest utilities, while considering additional substantial purchases of power from traditional hydro and new coal-fired sources, are planning to meet most new demands through non-traditional investments. These utilities are redirecting billions of dollars away from conventional energy sources and into conservation, load management, cogeneration, and small-scale, renewable resource alternatives.

Utilities are uniquely qualified to make sure that maximum efficiency improvements are implemented. Because of the nature of utility regulation, there are enormous opportunities for legislatures, community groups, and citizens to work with state regulators to implement sound energy policies. Utilities are accustomed to making multi-million-dollar investments in new generating capacity. In many instances it is much more cost-effective to invest this money in efficiency improvements than in new power plants.

Some utilities are offering cash rebates to consumers who purchase energy-efficient appliances. Others are providing free energy audits and below-market financing for investments in weatherization, large appliances, and other improvements that will reduce demand. Because these alternative investments can eliminate the need to invest in new generating capacity, the costs of these programs are shared by all ratepayers who benefit by not having to finance new generating capacity.

In addition to encouraging innovative alternative investments, utility regulators should remove any existing barriers to cogeneration. Electricity produced through cogeneration can require only one-half of the raw energy needed to generate electricity at a central station power plant. Cooperative arrangements between industry and utilities to increase cogeneration is a particularly appropriate way for many utilities to add new capacity; cogencrated electricity can be available in a short time and requires a relatively small capital investment.

Decreasing vulnerability to supply disruptions and increasing U.S. flexibility to respond to unanticipated events should be a central goal when planning new generating facilities. Large-scale centralized power facilities are not only an economic drain, they also increase a region's vulnerability to supply disruptions. Minor incidents at nuclear plants, fuel transportation disruptions, and other unpredictable events can cause serious temporary supply shortages. Small-scale, decentralized generating facilities that require lower capital costs and short lead times provide flexible energy systems capable of responding to changing needs and any number of uncertainties.

With full involvement of citizens, the help of state regulators, and leadership from those utilities already adapting to these new ideas, the economic crisis facing many utilities can be turned around. According to a 1983 study by the Congressional Research Service, utility load management programs alone could reduce electric demand by the equivalent of 124 large power plants over the next 15 years. Given the proper incentives, utilities can help in the transition to a future based on high efficiency and renewable energy sources.

Refocusing Federal Efforts. In its role as an energy promoter, the government has provided generous subsidies and tax incentives for the extraction of resources and production of power. Social, economic, and environmental considerations have often taken a back seat to the perceived energy needs of the country. All too often a "crisis mentality" has dominated federal energy policies. The oil shocks of the 1970s stimulated the creation of the Synthetic Fuels Corporation and the proposal for an Energy Mobilization Board with power to waive laws. Government policies that subsidize energy production, regulate prices and fuel use, and force commercialization of immature technologies have been the source of many energy problems. The government should play an active role in bringing the nation through a smooth and rapid transition to a sustainable energy future.

Recommendations

Increasing Energy Efficiency

During the coming decades the U.S. will be facing many new and urgent problems. The challenge facing the nation is to build a sustainable energy future based on energy efficiency and carefully planned renewable energy sources.

- Federal and state governments should develop successful strategies at all levels for shifting to an energy system based on high-efficiency and renewable resources.
- Federal subsidies for energy production should be removed; the full costs of energy production should be internalized; Congress should establish mandatory efficiency standards for autos, appliances, and buildings; and Congress should direct federal research and development efforts toward emerging renewable technologies and energy efficiency improvements, and also eliminate federal commercialization programs.

Strategies for the Transition

A rapid and smooth transition to a renewable energy future will alleviate many of the urgent problems associated with current energy use. Developing and implementing new and creative strategies to help through the transition will continue to be at the forefront of the energy agenda.

- U.S. energy policy should be changed so as to reduce international tensions; dependence on imported oil should be reduced; the export of nuclear reactors should be stopped; and policy should be adopted to halt the spread of plutonium throughout the world.
- Environmental hazards associated with energy production from both conventional and renewable sources should be minimized. This can be done by reducing the burning of fossil fuels, retrofitting existing fossil fuel facilities with state-of-the-art pollution control technology, and substituting low-sulfur coal where appropriate; substituting natural gas for coal and oil wherever practical and appropriate; strengthening environmental controls on uranium mining, milling, and mill waste disposal operations; reducing dependence on nuclear power while protecting local community interests against the hazards of nuclear technology; upgrading existing hydro-power facilities as an alternative to building new dams in those locations where rivers are

not being restored to free-flowing conditions; minimizing the cumulative impacts of multiple energy projects within single watersheds; and carefully assessing environmental impacts of energy efficiency and renewable energy technologies.

- The financial crisis currently threatening the electric utility industry should be averted by: redefining the role of both electric and gas utilities from the selling of power to providing more services; removing barriers to cogeneration; promoting investments in efficiency improvements; and encouraging investments in renewable energy sources and small-scale generating facilities, wherever appropriate.

5

Water Resources

The field of water resources is in a state of flux. In the past, water resource policy and politics have been defined by the free flow of federal dollars into structural water resource development projects, such as dams and canals. But the flow of federal dollars has faltered in recent years; the best dam sites have already been plugged with earth and concrete; and the public's preferences have shifted from water development to outdoor recreation and water quality. By the end of the century, if those trends continue, we can expect to see the focus of water policy shift further from development of new structures to the efficient management of existing facilities and supplies. Such a shift should take place as rapidly as possible because improved efficiency offers the least cost solution to water problems and minimizes the environmental impacts and social disruption involved in displacing people to build dams and canals. In this sense the most attractive approach to meet water needs is similar to the soft path to meet energy needs; namely, a path of better management of existing supply and increased efficiency in use wherever possible.

Over the course of a century and a half, federal water politics and practices developed piecemeal to meet the needs of a growing nation: settling the open spaces and stimulating commerce and industry. From the early 19th century to the middle decades of the 20th, water development programs were supported by a consensus favoring federal spending to subsidize commercial expansion and regional development. They were financed by massive transfers of wealth from developed to developing regions, transfers that were in turn sustained by the congressional pork barrel system.

Water resource policies evolved according to the dictates of political convenience rather than economic efficiency. Irrigation water, flood control structures, navigation improvements, and other project outputs were supplied to beneficiaries at little or no cost. Federal funds were spent on water projects with little regard for national economic efficiency and even less concern for environmental costs. Both federal projects and the water they supplied were undervalued and therefore overused. Demands for water projects rose to inflated levels to capture the subsidies. Society learned to count on federally financed structural, supply-side solutions to its water problems—and came to define its water needs in those terms.

Over the past decade, however, many of the factors that have defined and sustained the traditional approach to water resource management have begun to change.

An era of open-handed federal spending has been terminated by chronic federal budget deficits. Faced with cuts in domestic spending and sharp competition for increasingly scarce federal dollars, it has become more difficult for federal water projects to compete with other uses of public funds.

With the best sites for water projects already used, those remaining will be more expensive to develop and often more environmentally objectionable.

The established national political consensus in favor of using water project spending to subsidize regional economic development has fractured as the economic decline in the North and East has forced the issue of inter-regional inequity. No new consensus on the goals and mechanisms of water policy has been reached.

The growing public commitment to environmental values has introduced effective new political opposition to established water development practices. By questioning the economic justification of water projects and emphasizing the environmental and social costs of their construction, citizens have weakened the political consensus for water project spending and have eliminated over 150 unnecessary dam, channelization, and canal projects during the past decade.

The course of water resource policy through the end of the century seems likely to be influenced by a number of emerging factors.

- Demands for the traditional array of water projects will continue due to a growing population, an expanding economy, and further population shifts to the South and the West.
- There will be an ongoing need to protect environmental values from destructive water projects.
- The established patterns of water development will be challenged by increased competition for federal dollars, by inter-regional rivalries, and by growing public concern for environmental quality.
- Water projects that do get authorized are likely to be smaller in scale, oriented toward least-cost solutions, with intergovernmental and public-private cost-sharing and shorter payout periods.
- The country need not suffer a national water crisis before the end of the century and is not about to run out of water. There is plenty of water to meet present and future needs—even in the West—if it is managed wisely.
- Water will become more valuable as competition for existing supplies becomes more intense.
- Water policies of the rest of the century will have to accommodate increased concerns for environmental values and the rights of third-party users, those downstream in space or time. In-stream uses of water for recreation, fish and wildlife, aesthetic enjoyment, and other water quality considerations, and the issue of inter-generational equity will complicate the search for new management modes and allocation devices.

In summary, the water crisis of the '80s and '90s is likely to be a crisis of management rather than of absolute supply. The era of structural water resource development in this country is largely over, although there will be a continuing need to defend environmental values against poorly planned, economically unjustified water projects. The issues of the future will concern allocation of existing supplies and management of existing facilities, rather than major new capital construction. Thus, the major challenge of the next decade and a half will be to design the institutions and procedures necessary to make existing U.S. water resources and water management facilities meet society's changing economic and environmental needs.

Recommendations

User Charges and Cost-sharing

In the past, the decision to build water projects has been made with little concern for their economic efficiency. Potential beneficiaries have lobbied for federally funded water developments without regard for their true costs. As a result, society has overinvested in water development projects; public funds have been wasted on projects that will produce no net economic benefits to the nation; and environmental values have been sacrificed to uneconomical and unneeded water developments.

Society's interest in both economic efficiency and environmental quality can be protected by requiring those who benefit from federal water developments to repay the full costs of projects. Demand for projects would therefore reflect the discipline of the marketplace, rather than the undisciplined pursuit of subsidies. Benefits and costs—including environmental costs— would be carefully weighed. Project planning would focus on least-cost alternatives. Use of a realistic discount rate and a requirement for cost-sharing during construction would further restrict the demand for projects of excessive scale and extended pay-off periods.

- **The federal government should ensure that all categories of federal water projects are environmentally, socially, and economically sound. Establishment of the policy that users of water projects pay the full costs of construction, operation, and maintenance would help ensure this objective. Cost recovery should include external costs and interest charges that reflect the cost of long-term federal borrowing. Non-federal interests should be required to pay for most of the capital cost of the project during construction.**

Water Allocation

Stretching existing water supplies to meet future needs will be possible only if new institutional arrangements are developed for re-allocating water from low value to higher value uses. The price of water must rise to reflect its scarcity value and the marginal cost of new supplies.

Mechanisms must be developed for more freely transferring water among alternative users. Other offsetting mechanisms must be devised to protect the rights of third parties against damage resulting from water transfers. At the same time, existing institutional impediments to water transfers within a service system in both eastern and western states should be addressed.

Experience to date with a number of market and pseudo-market mechanisms has demonstrated that economic incentives will produce transfers of water from lower to higher value uses. But the same experience has also led observers to conclude that market mechanisms must be tailored to individual legal and geographic circumstances, and carefully limited to protect non-market values.

- **The federal government should actively support the development, testing, and evaluation of a variety of legal and institutional mechanisms for effecting water rights transfers. At the same time, however, to protect non-market, environmental values—including fish and wildlife, dispersed recreation, water quality, and aesthetic enjoyment—the workings of the market must be constrained or regulated.**

Conservation and Non-structural Solutions

A variety of non-structural alternatives has proven effective at solving water problems while reducing environmental damage and saving federal tax dollars. For example, flood control objectives can be accomplished through such non-structural alternatives as flood plain parks, zoning, flood-proofing or relocating structures out of the hazard area, and protection of watersheds and wetlands upstream. Navigation efficiency can be improved through scheduling of lockages, use of switchboats, and charging of user fees to constrain demand for costly lockage facilities. Recreation needs could be met by improving public access to streams and lakes and developing facilities at existing reservoirs.

Problems of water supply can be eased or solved entirely by making more efficient use of existing supplies—by water conservation. The potential for water conservation in the industrial, residential, and agricultural sectors is immense, especially in the most arid regions of the country. Irrigation accounts for 81 percent of the nation's water consumption, but 50 to 80 percent of that water is lost to leakage and evaporation before it reaches the crops. Much of that water could be saved. Subsidies for irrigation under agricultural tax laws contribute to the wastage. Municipal water systems across the nation lose an average of 12 percent of their water to leaks, with Boston recording losses of 35 percent. Residential use can be cut by more than half through a combination of simple conservation measures.

Over the rest of this century, water efficiency improvements offer the least-cost and most environmentally acceptable solution to problems of water supply. Water saved through increases in efficiency can be made available for other uses more quickly and at far lower unit cost than water supplied from new sources. But the potential for water conservation will not be fully realized until pricing policies and the chance to profit from water saved offer individual users economic incentives to conserve.

- Congress and the Administration should work to revise federal water planning procedures to insure that nonstructural alternatives are given fair consideration, and should support reforms in federal water pricing and supply contracts to provide financial incentives for water conservation.

In-stream Uses

In-stream uses of water include fish and wildlife propagation, recreation, and aesthetic enjoyment. Demand for these simple, collective values is growing extremely rapidly as the public both uses streams more often and attaches a higher value to that use. However, in-stream uses are frequently in conflict— legally and physically—with the individual, off-stream uses of water that have enjoyed legal recognition.

Under the appropriation doctrine of the western states, a water right exists only when water is diverted from a stream and put to beneficial use. Instream uses are usually left wholly unprotected. Under conditions of drought or over-appropriation, in-stream values, including fish and wildlife, are frequently damaged or destroyed. As competition for water intensifies, the conflict between in-stream and off-stream uses will become increasingly severe, and damage to in-stream values will become more common.

- Federal and state governments should make protection of in-stream values a major commitment over the next decade. The initial phase of that commitment should focus on expanding public awareness of the threats to in-stream values and establishing the intellectual and legal basis for securing state legislation to protect those values.

Federal Institutions and Procedures

In 1977, at the high point of federal spending on water resource projects, the four principal construction agencies were spending more than $3 billion per year. Projects were planned and approved without due consideration for national economic efficiency or environmental costs. Cost-sharing requirements varied widely among agencies and project purposes, inviting local sponsors to tailor projects to maximize the federal share. Artificially low discount rates understated the cost of water projects and led to facilities of excessive scale. Construction agencies both designed the projects and advised Congress and the Office of Management and Budget (OMB) on their worth.

It is time for a systematic revision of the rules of the game to correct past abuses and to design institutions that will efficiently serve current and future needs.

- Congress should pass legislation to de-authorize federal water resource projects that have been authorized for eight years or longer but are not yet under construction. Projects or segments less than one-half completed should be re-evaluated under revised benefit/cost procedures and using realistic discount rates.
- Congress should realign the missions of the three federal water resource construction agencies to emphasize management of existing facilities and de-emphasize capital construction. The Bureau of Reclamation should be assigned a new role as a water management agency, focusing on improving the efficiency of water use in the arid West. The water resources functions of the Soil Conservation Service should be substantially realigned, giving attention to water quality, especially non-point pollution, and abandoning dam building and channelization. The civil works functions of the Army Corps of Engineers should be redirected from capital construction of water development facilities to water management techniques, non-structural solutions for water problems, and operation and maintenance of the existing network of federal projects. Also, major water development agencies—the Army Corps of Engineers, the Bureau of Reclamation, and the Soil Conservation Service's small watershed program—should be consolidated for better coordination and efficient management.
- The discount rate used to evaluate the economic viability of water projects should be increased to reflect the average cost of long-term federal borrowing.
- The Principles and Guidelines for Water Resource Planning should be systematically revised and issued in the form of binding regulations.

- An independent review board should be established to evaluate the feasibility and worth of all federally funded water projects, separating responsibility for evaluation from responsibility for design, construction, and operation.

Groundwater

Nearly one-half of the nation's population relies on groundwater as its principal source of drinking water. In the West, groundwater has supported the rapid expansion of irrigation for nearly 20 years.

Future uses of groundwater are threatened by pollution and by excessive withdrawals, on both local and regional levels. In much of the arid West, groundwater is being "mined"—pumped out at rates that exceed natural recharge—lowering water tables, increasing pumping costs, reducing surface flows from springs and seeps, and in some cases causing cracking or subsidence of the land surface.

- **Each state should adopt comprehensive state groundwater management statutes that provide for: sustained-yield management of groundwaters; regulation of withdrawals by quotas or pump taxes; transfer of pumping quotas and sale of pumped water; a ban on mining of rechargeable aquifers; conjunctive management of surface and groundwaters; protection of groundwater quality against contamination; and coordinated management of inter-state aquifers.**
- **Federal, state, and local governments should integrate groundwater management into federal policy and planning so that groundwater supplies are protected and managed in conjunction with surface waters; federal water program benefits are denied to states that do not regulate groundwater withdrawals and fail to protect aquifers from contamination; and federal financing or assistance is withheld from projects that would damage water resources.**

Wetlands

Wetlands are both an extraordinarily valuable natural resource in their own right and a critical component of the larger water system. Wetlands moderate floods and droughts by absorbing flood peak flows and slowly releasing their waters through low-flow periods. Coastal wetlands protect human settlements by absorbing storm surges. Wetlands protect water quality by removing silt and harmful biological and chemical pollutants.

However, since the country's settlement, more than 50 percent of U.S. native wetlands have been destroyed. From the mid-1950s through the mid-1970s wetlands were lost to drainage and development at more than 500,000 acres per year. Federal programs to defend wetlands have helped slow the rate of loss, but have fallen short of providing the needed measure of protection. Water Bank contracts remain unrenewed for lack of funding. Funds available for wetlands purchases under the Wetlands Loan Act remain unspent. Meanwhile, federal tax laws subsidize the speculative drainage of wetlands for croplands and other development.

- Congress should sharply accelerate funding for the wetlands acquisition program; integrate wetlands and water quality protection into federal agricultural commodity programs so that farmers cropping newly drained wetlands would be ineligible for all federal agricultural loans and support payments; and amend federal tax laws to prohibit all deductions or credits for the expenses of preparing wetlands for development (including costs of purchase, clearing, drainage, and filling) and to provide tax benefits for wetlands conservation. Congress should also strengthen Section 404 of the Clean Water Act, by liberalizing the rules for citizens' suits, and requiring EPA to veto Section 404 permits involving unacceptable impacts on wetlands, wildlife, or water quality, such as large landfills in rivers.

Toxics and Pollution Control

In the decade and a half since the enactment of landmark environmental legislation, the items on the pollution control agenda have increased faster than they have diminished. Progress has been made in controlling some sources of pollution, though more slowly and with greater difficulty than expected a decade ago. Serious pollution problems remain unsolved, while new problems continue to arise.

Environmental regulation has worked in some areas, but progress often is excruciatingly slow. In many American cities air quality has stopped getting worse and started getting better since passage of the Clean Air Act. Yet more than half the population—140 million Americans—live in areas where air pollutants still exceed health standards for some part of the year. Some streams and rivers are markedly cleaner because of the regulation of municipal and industrial discharges. Yet since 1972 almost four times more of the area of lakes and reservoirs has degraded in quality than has improved. The bald eagle population has recovered due to a ban on DDT, but residues still persist in the food chain long after DDT use was banned. Limits on lead additives in gasoline have prevented hundreds of thousands of cases of lead poisoning in children, but hundreds of thousands more children could have been spared if lead phasedown had not been delayed.

Although progress has been made, most forms of pollution are not under control, and new problems continue to confront the nation. Also old problems, such as asbestos, dioxin, and PCBs, persist long after regulatory programs are initiated. And while the U.S. Environmental Protection Agency asserts a more optimistic view, there is much evidence that compliance with even those pollution control standards that are in effect is poor. Monitoring, inspection, and enforcement have been sporadic and inconsistent. If there is no change in the status quo during the next several decades, the next generation will inherit a land that is neither clean nor safe, and far more polluted than at present.

If any lesson is to be derived from the mistakes of the past, it is that it is cheaper to prevent environmental contamination than it is to clean it up once it has occurred. Unfortunately, the country has not done a very good job of either prevention or cleanup. Failure to prevent damage to valuable resources represents a poor economic choice that in the long run will be more costly to society than preventive regulation.

Shared Principles

The responses to these complex challenges flow from a set of principles shared by all. The fundamental need is to find and implement the means by which a complex industrial society can function and grow without destroying or depleting the ecosystems that sustain it.

Pollution is destructive and the damage is cumulative. It is neither efficient nor wise to allow essential, commonly held, life-sustaining resources—air, water, and land—to be used without cost on a first-come, first-served basis, in a manner that destroys the utility of the resource for others. Such a system is cheap for the first user but very expensive for society. It is profoundly wasteful.

The goals of environmental regulation are based on sound economic principles—correcting for the fact that the private market does not provide financial incentives to reduce "externalities" such as pollution. Actions that contaminate the nation's natural resources impose costs upon all citizens, and these costs are no less real because they involve damage to resources that had always been free.

Wealth includes not only goods and leisure, but health, safety, and a land worth living on and passing along to the next generation. These are real goods that are of value to all, but their preservation and enhancement require governmental action. Individuals are severely limited in their ability to protect themselves against the costs and risks of pollution, particularly when they are exposed to toxic substances. Environmental regulation to protect health, safety, and the land—part of the nation's real wealth—improves economic welfare and increases economic efficiency.

Government can also seek to minimize involuntary exposure to risk by enforcing a liability system that compensates individuals for their exposure to risk, thus reducing incentives for risk generation. Experience with toxic tort actions to date suggests that the difficulties of proving causal connections and the enormous transaction costs of litigation will reduce the effectiveness of this option as a means of minimizing risks by compensating victims. Despite its limitations, a strong liability system should be maintained to deal with instances where government regulation fails to protect individuals from being harmed by pollutants.

Regulation

Federal pollution control laws are enforced through regulations that set forth detailed and specific requirements. The concept is simple: the government seeks a certain result—reduced pollution. To achieve that result the government tells polluters precisely what they must do and then checks to see that they do it.

This system of broad legislative commands, implemented through detailed regulations, has many deficiencies. It can be inflexible, dauntingly complex to understand, difficult to administer, enforce, or even comply with. Regulations often turn out to be pierced by unforseseen loopholes. But the regulations are necessary to protect people and the environment they inhabit.

Pollution control sometimes involves new technology. There are enormous gaps in our knowledge about the sources, extent, and effects of pollution. Around those gaps swirl controversies that delay and weaken regulation, even after Congress has decided to require EPA to proceed in the face of uncertainty to prevent possible harm.

The regulation of toxic chemicals is a compelling example. A study by a committee of the National Academy of Sciences concluded that Americans are exposed to about 65,000 chemicals, of which about two percent have been thoroughly tested to determine whether and how they may affect human health. EPA is responsible for the regulation of thousands of these chemicals under nine separate statutes:* The Agency has been unable to do the job. Its progress in regulating toxics has been halting at best, and achieved generally under the compulsion of environmental lawsuits.

The regulation of toxics requires EPA to protect widely dispersed populations exposed to minute quantities of large numbers of chemicals in many media (air, drinking water, food, etc.) over long periods of time. EPA has approached the problem statute by statute, medium by medium, chemical by chemical. The standards for protection are different under each statute. The industries, populations, and chemicals have effects that overlap but are not identical. The toxic pollution eliminated from one medium is sometimes shifted to another—yesterday's toxic discharge into a river sometimes becomes today's hazardous waste in a dump or tomorrow's air and groundwater pollution.

In many instances, industries believe that it is in their economic interest to delay or weaken regulations. Indeed, for any particular regulation, the stakes for the regulated are far higher than they are for any individual member of the public. EPA has had to fight the same battles in implementing legislation that Congress fought in writing it, but in a less public, more technical setting, where the infinitely greater resources of industry often overwhelm environmental interests.

EPA has increasingly asked: "How do we decide what environmental risks are acceptable and which we should seek to reduce first?" The answer of many in industry and most economists is: calculate the costs of controls and impose only those requirements that produce benefits that exceed the costs of obtaining them.

Cost-benefit analysis is a tool aimed at making rational decisions. When confined to economic values, however, experience has shown that cost-benefit analysis usually overestimates compliance costs by not considering technological innovation. Similarly, these analyses underestimate benefits because of the difficulty of quantifying them. Moreover, too little is known to be able to say with certainty how great that risk is; yet past experience has demonstrated that it is appropriate to adhere to the

*The Clean Air Act, the Clean Water Act, the Federal Insecticide, Fungicide and Rodenticide Act, the Food, Drug and Cosmetic Act (pesticide residues), the Ocean Dumping Act, the Resources Conservation and Recovery Act, Superfund, the Toxic Substances Control Act, and the Safe Drinking Water Act.

adage "better safe than sorry," even if predictable costs purchase benefits that cannot be predicted with certainty. One additional problem with cost-benefit analysis is that it tends to reduce the environmental debate to one involving technical numbers and thus becomes a debate that is difficult for the concerned citizen to understand, much less participate in.

There are practical difficulties in complete reliance on cost-benefit analysis as well. If specific pollution-reduction objectives are replaced by relative objectives based on comparative costs, the regulatory process will get bogged down in an endless debate over whether any specific regulatory scheme is "worth it." Reliance on technical economic analyses to determine EPA's regulatory agenda will sharply reduce or eliminate judicial review of agency decisions. Lacking the technical assistance to rebut every assumption contained in a cost-benefit analysis, the public will be forced to leave regulatory decisions to the "experts." Without public accountability, the experts have little incentive to make tough regulatory decisions.

Ecomomic analysis is an important and potentially powerful tool, but since it has the potential to be seriously misused, continuing care must be exercised in its use. Analysis of cost effectiveness or of "comparative risk" should not, for instance, be used to administratively remake congressionally enacted public health and environmental decisions.

Reform of Regulation

It is possible to reform the regulatory system without abolishing it. However, regulatory reform has often been a euphemism for less regulation and more pollution. Specific requirements have the virtue of concreteness, and, at least theoretically, predictability. Then, as long as financial resources are available, it should be possible to find out whether industry is complying.

Many of the "reforms" that are seriously proposed for the regulatory system would either make it more difficult for EPA to issue regulations or allow regulated industries (or the state) more flexibility. In light of the consistent difficulty EPA has had in fulfilling its legal obligation to regulate polluters, environmentalists have been reluctant even to experiment with approaches that might worsen the situation by giving polluters flexibility to do less. Instead, environmentalists have advocated amendments that would make the congressional mandate to EPA more specific and explicit. They have argued that such provisions are necessary to force EPA to act, while realizing that such specifics also limit the agency's ability to respond to legitimate claims of special circumstances.

Toward New Approaches

There are serious problems with attempting to use regulations to control pollution, yet given the critical need, they must continue to be used. Reforming the regulatory process to make it more effective must be a continuing effort, though with care that "reform" not be used as a technique to loosen controls.

EPA's chemical-by-chemical approach to hazardous waste regulation is so cumbersome that it has paralyzed the regulatory process. Government must move to control those groups of chemical "cousins" whose toxicity and other properties are closely related. Rigid insistence on reams of studies for each separate chemical within groups of cousins has proven to be unworkable.

New approaches must include increased emphasis on source reduction. Minimizing the generation of polluting wastes is ultimately vital to protecting the health of the people, the economy, and the environment. Source reduction and other management techniques are now in use in many companies, individual states, and foreign countries. Many fall under the following broad categories:

Housekeeping. Review of process efficiency and practices that may reveal unnecessary or unintended by-products that can easily be collected.

Substitution. Use of alternative materials may yield the same quality product while producing a non-hazardous or more easily recyclable waste stream.

End of Process Reclamation. On- or off-site recovery of re-usable and marketable materials, which can reduce waste volumes and decrease disposal and material expenses.

Waste Exchanges. Re-use of one firm's waste by another firm as an input for a different production process.

Increased emphasis on these approaches should include regulatory incentives for their use, as well as efforts by private industry to demonstrate the viability of affordable waste disposal and reduction alternatives.

Recommendations

Hazardous Waste

The United States produces over 254 million tons of hazardous waste per year (more than one ton per person), far more than anyone realized even a year ago. Nearly a decade after the passage of legislation to control the disposal of hazardous wastes, EPA is still struggling to implement it. The only certainties are that most dumps and storage facilities leak toxics into the air, earth, and groundwater, and all will leak sooner or later. All too often in emergency situations workers, neighbors, and emergency service teams are without information they need for evaluating or effectively coping with possible risk. Out of approximately 5,000 active hazardous waste facilities, only 380 final permits had been issued by April 1985, and many hazardous waste streams escape all regulation. Long-term solutions to the hazardous waste problem has not even been remotely approached. As a consequence of careless disposal of wastes in the past, over 20,000 sites around the country are suspected of containing abandoned toxic wastes. It will cost at least $12 billion and take a decade or longer just to clean up the 1,800 worst sites.

- Congress should approve a five-year, $12 billion extension of Superfund to move the cleanup ahead. The extension should include specific enforceable deadlines for EPA action, broad coverage of natural resource damage, guarantees that citizens have a right to know what kind of toxic chemicals are being stored in, processed in, or moved through their communities, and a workable system to assure that victims of hazardous waste contamination are not left without recourse or assistance.
- Congress should appropriate substantially increased funds for EPA's implementation of the newly strengthened Resources Conservation and Recovery Act.
- Government should develop and adopt measures that encourage the use of technologies and processes that minimize or eliminate the generation of hazardous waste.
- Government, industry, and environmental groups, should cooperate in an effort to spur development of source reduction and alternative waste mangement technologies.

- EPA should move to regulate groups of closely related chemical "cousins" since the chemical-by-chemical approach has proven unworkable.

Groundwater Protection

Hazardous wastes, pesticides, and over 100,000 leaking industrial lagoons and underground storage tanks have contaminated a significant amount of the nation's groundwater. Tens of thousands of wells have been closed, millions of people drink water containing toxics, and no one can say with certainty which aquifers are contaminated. Once contaminated, groundwater is difficult and costly to clean up, even when contamination can be detected. The combination of depletion of groundwater supplies due to increased use and widespread contamination of these supplies is a recipe for disaster.

Effective implementation and enforcment of the pesticide and hazardous waste laws, while crucial, is not enough.

- Congress should pass a strong safe drinking water law that sets deadlines for the adoption and enforcement of maximum contaminant levels for toxics in drinking water (no such standards now exist for most toxics) and that requires anyone responsible for contaminating drinking water supplies to provide alternative supplies.
- EPA and the U.S. Geological Survey should immediately initiate a comprehensive groundwater mapping and monitoring program and carry it out in cooperation with the states.

Pesticides

News coverage of the terrible effects of ethylene dibromide (EDB) in groundwater and methyl isocyanate at Bhopal, India, have focused the attention of the entire nation on the dangers inherent in the manufacture and use of deadly pesticides. Pesticides, herbicides, and fungicides are created to kill living organisms and are used on almost everything we eat. One-third to one-half of our food contains pesticide residues. More than twelve years ago, Congress instructed EPA to regulate the safety of newly introduced pesticides and review those already in use. But EPA has not done so. Products for which there is animal test data showing that the products are carcinogens, mutagens, or teratogens remain in widespread use. Only about ten percent of the pesticides in use have been adequately tested to see if they cause cancer or birth defects.

While pesticide use has increased ten-fold in the last 40 years, the same proportion of the nation's crops are still lost to pests. The expense of heavy chemical use is an enormous burden to many farmers.

- Congress should amend the Federal Insecticide, Fungicide and Rodenticide Act (FIFRA) to set deadlines for EPA safety review of existing pesticides and impose a sunset date beyond which a pesticide may not be used if it has not undergone complete safety tests.
- Congress should amend the Federal Food, Drug and Cosmetic Act to require EPA to use realistic health-based standards for the amount of pesticide residue permitted on food, eliminating all exceptions such as that which existed for EDB.
- Congress should increase federal support for research and demonstration of non-chemical and reduced-chemical pest control methods.

Surface Water

The nation has made some progress in the control of surface water pollution under the Clean Water Act, such as the cleanup of Lake Erie, but major problems remain. The law has not been effectively enforced, and some polluters dump toxics directly into surface water or into municipal sewage treatment plants that are not equipped to handle them. New development results in the degradation of pristine streams and destruction of critical fish and wildlife habitat.

A 1984 Conservation Foundation report estimates that over half of the nation's water pollutants come from non-point sources, particularly unregulated stormwater runoff from agricultural lands and city streets. Eighteen thousand lakes and tens of thousands of miles of rivers and streams have been polluted. Present law does not address non-point sources

- Congress should amend the Clean Water Act to control non-point sources of surface water pollution.
- Congress should appropriate funds to expedite EPA's implementation and enforcement of regulations requiring dischargers of toxic effluents to treat those effluents before they reach municipal sewage treatment facilities.
- Since pesticides are a major non-point source of water pollution, government bodies should encourage the development and implementation of non-chemical pest management techniques.

Air Pollution

Air pollution can be controlled, and in some cases has been, but in most cases performance has fallen short of what the country is capable of attaining.

Acid rain caused by powerplants, smelters, and to a lesser extent automobile emissions threatens lakes, streams, roads, and buildings. Combined with other pollutants, it reduces forest growth and affects crops. Control of acid rain is a critical priority. The nation will eventually act to control it. However, if present delays continue, future generations will look back and wonder how the country could have waited and watched the destruction go on for so long.

Industry legally discharges into the air hundreds of toxic chemicals known to cause acute and chronic illnesses, including cancer. A recent EPA study concluded that several dozen of these emissions may cause up to 2,000 cases of cancer each year. The Clean Air Act requires EPA to regulate such emissions, but in 14 years they have regulated but five, and those only partially.

As noted in the report on the urban environment, most Americans live in cities, towns, or suburbs—close together—and they spend much of their time indoors. It is quite possible that the average American's exposure to toxics has as much to do with the products used and the way they are used as with pollution caused by industrial activity. Stoves, furnaces, fireplaces, construction materials, furnishings, paints, cleaning products, and pesticides, as well as smoking, may all be sources of significant health risks in the home and workplace, and in many rural areas the increased use of wood stoves has created a new health hazard. There is little hard data on the extent of these risks, and the Office of Management and Budget has undercut all efforts to collect data. Reduction of these risks, if they are significant, will require a very different approach than that used to control pollution from major industrial sources.

Finally, there is mounting evidence that profound changes are occurring in the basic make-up of the atmosphere because of pollution on earth. The amount of carbon dioxide in the atmosphere has increased by nearly 30 percent since the start of the industrial revolution. This trend is accelerating due to the widespread use of fossil fuels and the destruction of tropical forests. Many scientists believe increased levels of carbon dioxide in the atmosphere will have profound effects on the world climate in the next several decades.

But it is not only carbon dioxide that is increasing. Trace gases such as methane, nitrous oxide, and carbon monoxide are rising and levels of sulfur, phosphorus, and nitrogen oxide are also rising. Scientists do not know what will happen as a result of these changes, but they warn that by the time we do know it will be too late to reverse the process.

- Congress should pass acid rain legislation requiring a 50 percent reduction in sulfur emissions and providing assurances that the costs of the program will be fairly apportioned.
- Congress should amend the Clean Air Act to impose enforceable deadlines for EPA action on specified toxic air pollutants.
- EPA should take immediate action to reduce dangerous particulate emissions from diesels and wood-burning stoves and furnaces.
- Congress should require EPA, in cooperation with the National Academy of Sciences, to make an expeditious and complete review of the problem of indoor air pollution, and develop model building code provisions for adoption by the states to deal with indoor air quality problems.
- Congress should require EPA, in cooperation with other nations, to conduct a comprehensive study of the extent, causes, and potential consequences of the buildup of pollutants in the atmosphere.

Genetic Engineering

The modification of basic life forms holds tremendous promise. It may enable mankind to improve agricultural production, reduce pollution, control disease, and develop new clean sources of energy. According to ecologists, however, there may also be risks that the world is poorly equipped to understand in releasing new life forms into the environment. The federal government has poured money into research on genetic engineering, but almost none of it has gone to assess potential risks. The government's approach to the growing genetic engineering industry has been to look only at products, not at the production process or the potential for accidental release of gene engineered products.

- Government should adopt a policy of no release into the environment of gene engineered products without a full understanding of the potential effects.

- Environmental scientists should initiate a joint effort with academic and industry scientists to develop, and government and industry should fund, a research agenda on the potential risks of genetic engineering.
- EPA and the Occupational Safety and Health Administration (OSHA) should develop standards for the design and operation of facilities using or manufacturing gene engineered organisms on a commercial scale.

Institutional Resources

The budget deficit of the United States is a serious problem which must be brought under control. Yet the future health of the nation's citizens, as well as that of the economy and the environment, are in serious jeopardy due to the continued fouling of the environment. A major factor in the failure of the United States to achieve the progress promised in its environmental laws has been the mismatch between the work required and the resources available. The environmental agencies, and in particular EPA and its counterparts in the states, have suffered from a chronic shortage of resources. The operating budget of EPA has declined since 1980 and now stands, in real dollars, where it was in 1975, when the agency had no responsibility for toxic substances or hazardous wastes. EPA is a small agency—it has one-tenth as many employees as the Department of Agriculture—yet EPA is charged with enforcing laws that affect every phase of human life. Even though the budget of EPA ought to be increased, the elimination of subsidies, as proposed throughout this document, would offset these increases.

EPA shares responsibility with state pollution control agencies. If states do not carry out the laws, the laws do not work; but the program the states implement represents national policy. EPA grants to the states have been reduced, and that is crippling their programs.

- Congress should accept the implications of the programs it has enacted and give EPA the increased resources necessary to do the job, including funds for increased state grants.

The Information Gap

Perhaps the greatest obstacle to effective pollution control is the lack of solid information. There is shockingly little data about what contaminants are in the air, water, land, and food, and between 1981 and 1985 the amount of testing and monitoring has decreased.

Many of the 65,000 commercial chemicals identified by the National Academy of Sciences are currently being marketed, yet for most of them there is little or no data available on their potential to cause cancer, birth defects, or chronic diseases. A recent National Academy of Sciences report concluded that sufficient information to complete a health hazard assessment is available for less than two percent of commercial chemicals. Exposure data are quite poor and most testing for chronic effects has focused on cancer rather than reproductive and neurological disorders or their chronic effects. Almost nothing is known about the synergistic effects of exposure to combinations of chemicals.

Where clear facts are available, as in the case of lead in gasoline, it is only because Congress has chosen to regulate in the face of uncertainty. Then the data generated through the regulatory experience has demonstrated the worth of even stricter regulation. More often, however, lack of information has stymied regulation and may continue to do so because government research on environmental and health effects has been sharply curtailed. This is, in real terms, investment in ignorance futures.

- Congress should appropriate higher amounts, and industry should increase its expenditures, for expanded research on health, safety, and pollution control technology.
- The President should restore the Council on Environmental Quality to its proper place as an advisor to the President and a collector, coordinator, and purveyor of environmental, safety, and health data.
- Right-to-know legislation making information available to neighbors, workers, and those in emergency service teams ought to be passed by federal, state, and local governments.
- Environmental organizations, industry, and leading academic institutions should cooperate to create an independent institution for research on environmental hazards.

The gaps in knowledge about toxic pollutants have been highlighted by the ghastly incident in Bhopal. The public asked about the risks of such a disaster occurring in the U.S. and found that no one knows the answer. There is no inventory of all the sites and processes that involve the manufacture, storage, or transportation of substances that could cause widespread death or injury in case of an accident. EPA does not have and cannot quickly collect data on the number, causes, and consequences of accidents that have occurred. There is confusion about which statutes apply and how large the loopholes are, such as that for "intermediates"—chemicals used in the manufacture of other chemicals.

- **EPA should immediately develop an inventory of sites and processes that could cause death, injury, or serious environmental damage off-site in the event of an accident.**
- **EPA and OSHA should immediately launch a fugitive emissions and accident enforcement campaign.**

Institutional Reform

Most federal environmental policy has been concocted in a cauldron of controversy. Bitter fights in Congress (often leading to deceptively lopsided votes in favor of environmental legislation), convoluted regulatory battles, and massive litigation have been major ingredients in the development and implementation of programs that should represent an overwhelmingly popular consensus. Increasingly, the parties to these disputes have recognized that the costs of litigation, to themselves and to the nation, are very high and have made tentative moves toward negotiation and compromise as an alternative.

This forum—the negotiating table—provides opportunity for development of regulatory experiments, but several conditions are essential. The parties must have some confidence in each other's good faith; each must have some power in the situation; all affected parties must be legitimately represented; and each must be convinced of the integrity of the federal institutions that participate in the process. Negotiation efforts are not, however, intended as a substitute for the resolution of serious public issues, for which continued public debate is essential.

- **Industry and concerned citizen groups should find discrete and specific opportunities for negotiation and experimentation.**
- **EPA, in cooperation with industry and citizen groups, should undertake experiments with the use of compliance incentives and market-based regulations.**

Tools for Citizens

The style of citizen participation and public interest activism that is a leading feature in American respresentative government includes four components: the use of information to promote public awareness of environmental issues; willingness and ability to challenge the "official version" of the facts; effective mobilization of grassroots pressure to influence Congress, state legislatures, and local government; and use of litigation to force government to fully implement legislation, even if there is strong political pressure to delay or soften it.

- **Citizens should have the opportunity to participate in the decisionmaking process of government and industry in order to ensure continued progress against pollution. Pollution control laws should provide mechanisms and rewards to citizens to help with enforcement.**

7

Wild Living Resources

From the inspirational majesty of the soaring bald eagle, symbol of the nation, to the unseen labors of the earthworm readying soil for the renewed life of spring, wild plants and animals are the ultimate resources upon which human life depends. At the same time every human activity, whether it be agriculture, industry, energy production, recreation, or finance, produces—directly or indirectly—some sort of impact on some wild living resource somewhere. As a result, the recommendations made in other chapters are likely to have important benefits for wildlife and wild plant conservation as well. This chapter focuses on those programs, policies, and initiatives that have living resource conservation as their primary purpose, or that have the most significant impact on living resource conservation.

There exists among the public a great diversity of views as to the principal objectives of wild living resources conservation. To ecologically-minded conservationists, wild living species in their natural communities represent opportunities to advance human understanding of nature, of evolution, of behavior, and ultimately of humanity itself. To others, wild living resources are essentially no different from other resources; the purpose of conserving them is to assure a continuous supply of the goods that can be derived from them and to maximize the income those goods produce, or as gene pools for enhancing future agricultural products or creating new medicines. Others emphasize the non-commercial utilization of at least some wild living resources, believing that the principal object of their conservation is to provide the recreational pleasures of chase and conquest in the sports of hunting and fishing. Without exhausting the full range of views, still others see in wild living resources fellow beings who are objects of awe, inspiration, beauty, and respect.

In the face of such disparate views, consensus on many issues of wild living resource conservation has often been elusive. Yet it is possible to identify certain shared convictions that give substance to the principle of wise use that must govern our relationship to all resources.

Conservation of Biological Diversity

The first shared goal must be the conservation of biological diversity—the immense variety and abundance of plant and animal life—by avoiding the unnecessary extinction of living species. The world of today faces the immediate threat of a staggering loss of wild species, unequalled in previous human history and perhaps in prehistoric times. A burgeoning human population and its attendant expansion into hitherto sparsely populated areas threatens to destroy the biological building blocks that are necessary for sustainable development. The plight of such species as the bald eagle, the rhinoceros, and the mountain gorilla are well known, but they represent just the tip of an iceberg of impending biological catastrophe. Even in our own already developed nation, wild plants and animals are still being lost, or threatened with loss, as a result of inadequate development planning and insufficient conservation of resources. Because of its irreversibility, prevention of species extinction as a result of human activity must be viewed as a fundamental shared goal.

Natural Habitat Restoration

Few of the potential values of wild living resources can be realized in laboratory or zoo-like environments. They can be realized most effectively by conserving natural habitats. Indeed, it is the destruction of natural habitats that is the major cause of endangerment for most species today. Thus a second important shared goal is to foster programs and policies that will contribute to the maintenance or restoration of areas of natural habitat.

The values of wild living organisms are not contained by national boundaries. From the raucous honking formations of geese to the delicate orange and black monarch butterflies, many species migrate across or live astride such borders. The areas of highest biological diversity—tropical moist forests and coral reefs—lie largely outside U.S. jurisdiction. Therefore, the goals of preventing extinction and protecting habitat must be addressed in both international and domestic arenas.

Notwithstanding the importance of the maintenance or restoration of natural habitats, it is clear that vast portions of the landscape are already radically altered from their natural condition and will remain so far into the foreseeable future. But these areas nonetheless still have living resource values, and opportunities often exist to enhance and advance those values and prevent further deterioration. Two other principles must guide efforts to realize these opportunities. The first is that diversity should be promoted, primarily because it offers the promise of maintaining the broadest array of living resources values, from harvesting to aesthetic appreciation. The corollary principle is that actions that tend to preclude or foreclose particular species or values should be discouraged. Thus the notion of avoiding wherever possible decisions that altogether eliminate one or more species from local areas, even though the species may exist elsewhere, should also be generally embraced. Both of these principles apply within the country as well in in the activities of American public and private institutions abroad.

Cooperative Wildlife Management

Although preservation of pristine habitat conditions is the basic ingredient for maintaining biological diversity, cooperative wildlife management and research can also do much to prevent extinction of threatened or endangered species. One such species is the grizzly bear, which is threatened in the United States (except in Alaska). Only 600 to 800 animals now survive south of the Canadian border, where up to 100,000 lived early in the nineteeth century.

Grizzly bear conservation is complicated because of the species' very low reproductive rate, its need for large areas of protected and relatively undisturbed habitat, its ability to inflict human injury, and its habit of roaming freely across areas managed by several federal or state agencies as well as intermingled private lands. But a federal-state Interagency Grizzly Bear Committee has given cohesive coordination and direction to grizzly management, research, and policy. Increased law enforcement efforts in the Yellowstone ecosystem to combat illegal killing of the animals, and a reward of up to $15,000 offered by the National Audubon Society for information leading to the arrest and conviction of grizzly poachers, have also helped to produce an encouraging result: there have been no confirmed illegal killings in the Yellowstone region during the past two years. Instead of the predictions of grizzly extinction in the continental United States, there is now hope that eventual recovery of the species may be possible, despite the formidable odds.

Efforts on behalf of the endangered whooping crane have been more successful. In the late 1940s only one flock of fewer than 20 whooping cranes was left in the world, and no one even knew where the whoopers went to lay their eggs. After Canadian and U.S. researchers succeeded in discovering a breeding area in northern Canada's Wood Buffalo National Park, research resulted in a captive breeding program conducted by the U.S. Fish and Wildlife Service. A foster parenting program was also started, using wild sandhill cranes to hatch and raise whooper chicks. An additional benefit has been that through the influence of the sandhill crane foster parents, the new flocks of whoopers have added a second migration route, further broadening the chances of survival. The whooping crane population has now increased to more than 150 birds and is continuing to grow. The purchase of Aransas National Wildlife Refuge in Texas to protect whooping crane wintering grounds has been an essential component of the recovery program.

Importance of Plant Diversity

As a final observation, it should be noted that until recently plants, invertebrates, and certain other groups of wild living resources have been almost completely neglected by all parties involved—government, conservation organizations, and the public. One has only to consider the role that plants living in tropical moist forests play in modern medicine. More than a fourth of all pharmaceuticals are based on these genetic resources, of which two-thirds have yet to be classified. With a growing public consciousness, this situation is now changing, but these living resources still do not receive consideration commensurate with their ecological importance or, often, the degree of the threat to their survival.

With these basic principles as a foundation, the question must be addressed: What more can be done through both government and private activity to further the cause of wild living resource conservation? In approaching this question it is useful to distinguish three quite different roles that government plays. First, government is itself responsible for the management and implementation of conservation programs, such as state management programs for resident wildlife refuges. Second, it is responsible for the building of roads, dams, and schools, and other development activities that often have major negative impacts on wild living resources and their habitats. Government's third role is to influence private activity, either promoting it through subsidies or tax incentives, or restraining it through direct regulatory programs.

Recommendations

Conservation Programs

Historically, wild living resource conservation programs have been built upon very narrow and limited financial bases. Recently, a trend to broaden these bases has begun, principally utilizing the mechanism of state income tax check-offs. A corollary objective of these efforts is to stabilize state agency funding as it expands so that future cutbacks and program disruptions do not occur. Some states have established successful fish and wildlife endowment funds that are proving useful in preventing drastic fluctuations in agency funding.

- State wild living resources agencies should expand their revenue bases beyond traditional sources and utilize such expanded revenues for broadened conservation programs; public interest organizations and concerned citizens should encourage, promote, and actively assist these efforts.

Endangered plant conservation has been sorely neglected by the federal government and most states. Though the Smithsonian Institution in 1975 identified a comprehensive list of some 3,000 U.S. plant species—roughly a tenth of the nation's native flora—likely to need the protection of the Endangered Species Act, fewer than 100 of them have yet been given that protection. Plants comprise the vast bulk of the so-called "candidate species" awaiting the Act's protection, yet at current listing rates a quarter century will be needed to complete action on the more than 1,000 species that comprise the top priority of the candidate list. Most states are wholly without any endangered plant conservation program, only 16 have entered into plant conservation cooperative agreements with the U.S. Fish and Wildlife Service under Section 6 of the Endangered Species Act, and many of those receive essentially no federal matching grants. Both state and federal plant conservation programs are also restricted by ineffective enforcement measures. Commitment to the preservation of biological diversity requires that serious efforts be directed toward bolstering the fledgling programs that address this pressing need.

- **The endangered species programs of the state and federal governments should increase their commitment of resources to the requirements of endangered plant and plant habitat conservation.**
- **Listing should be accelerated so that the existing backlog of candidate species, mostly plants, will be completed within a decade.**
- **Matching grants for state endangered species program cooperative agreements should be restored to at least the average program level of 1977, when the initial implementation of Section 6 of the Endangered Species Act began.**

Development Programs

For much of its history, government filled its conservation and its development roles seemingly unaware of their potential for conflict. Slowly, as recognition of this conflict grew, efforts were undertaken to temper the development activities of government so as not to impinge unduly on its conservation responsibilities. Today, two distinct approaches are used. One relies upon full disclosure of the potential environmental impacts of government actions with a view to ameliorating their adverse effects. The unstated premise of this approach, embodied in the National Environmental Policy Act and many state counterpart statutes, is that there is a limited public tolerance for government actions that exact a major environmental price. If forced to disclose what the environmental price of a planned action will be, the agencies of government may be deterred from those actions that cross the limits of public acceptability.

The second approach relies upon explicitly stated standards. These vary in formulation from the very general to the reasonably specific. Looking to the future requires that the adequacy of the standards now in place be assessed, including their enforceability, the need to develop standards where none now exist, and the possibility of broadening the alternative approach of public disclosure.

Although there have been many recent efforts to encourage the development of conservation plans for wild living resources (e.g., endangered species recovery plans under the Endangered Species Act, public lands wildlife conservation plans under the Sikes Act, nongame conservation plans under the Nongame Act, and comprehensive fish and wildlife plans under the Dingell-Johnson and Pittman-Robertson Acts), a major potential benefit of such planning has yet to be realized. That is, such plans can be rendered ineffective by actions of agencies beyond the effective influence of living resource planners. Unless they can be made effective, these plans have greatly diminished utility.

To make such a system workable, the planning process, and the plan approval step in particular, must provide for full consideration not only of the conservation values but also of other social values that may be affected by the plan. The type of planning that is required is complex, and agencies must be given sufficient time and resources to develop valid information on which to build. Nevertheless, in looking to the future, high priority must be given to better integration of the conservation planning efforts now being encouraged with the environmental standards restricting government development actions. It is also abundantly clear that development activities abroad, whether undertaken by private interests or promoted by government aid, can have major adverse impacts on living resources. Mechanisms to temper and restrain those activities to protect environmental values are necessary as they have been within the United States.

- **The U.S. government must recognize an obligation to monitor and, where necessary, control the harmful environmental impacts of its actions and those of U.S. based multi-national corporations operating in developing nations and on the high seas insofar as those actions affect biological diversity.**

Government Influences

The third role of government that can be distinguished is an indirect one. In this role, government does not itself undertake development activities. It does, however, substantially influence the development actions of a myriad of private actors in the national economy. The means of exerting this influence are many. They include tax policy, price supports, loan guarantees, insurance, and numerous other types of incentives and disincentives, as well as direct regulation. The private activities that are encouraged or discouraged by such policies can directly affect resource conservation.

Government, through a variety of open and hidden subsidies, often offers incentives to development that are inconsistent with conservation objectives. With elimination of such subsidies in areas of special ecological significance, such areas are less likely to be destroyed. This straightforward principle is reflected in the recent coastal barrier islands legislation, but it need not be limited to undeveloped coastal barrier islands. It could be made equally applicable to other areas of special ecological significance, such as wetlands, lands adjacent to national parks, endangered species critical habitats, and areas of special importance to migratory birds (the authority to designate such areas and provide special protection for them is provided by the U.S.-U.S.S.R migratory bird treaty, but it has yet to be implemented). The virtue of this approach is that it joins conservation considerations with economic concerns about the inefficiencies of government subsidies and with the larger public desire for less government.

- **Congress should expand the principle provided by the recent coastal barrier islands legislation as a way of discouraging unsound development in areas of special value for wild living resource conservation.**

8

Private Lands and Agriculture

Privately held lands, including farmlands, range, forests, wetlands, and mining lands, can present management problems that go beyond the boundary of ownership. Landowner's decisions can create off-site costs to society, which are subsequently addressed by government spending programs. Farmers and ranchers, for example, own more of the land resource base than any other single group in the nation. How farmers use their land, and how federal programs and federal tax policies influence certain agricultural uses of land affect the quality of soil and water. While most farmers and ranchers are responsible stewards of the resource base, fluctuating farm income and other economic pressures can cause them to abandon conservation practices.

Topsoil erosion and the non-agricultural conversion of prime farmland are major problems on America's private lands, and analyses show that other non-urban private land is diminishing. On-farm effects of erosion can be masked temporarily on deep topsoils by increased use of chemicals, but in areas with shallow topsoils, excessive rates of erosion can lead to rapidly reduced yields. Erosion from private lands contributes to the sedimentation of the nation's waterways and carries fertilizer and pesticides from farms to streams, rivers, and lakes. Unwise and inadequately regulated land management practices are serious contributors to pollution of water supplies.

Federal and state programs have not generally been very effective in dealing with the problems associated with destructive cultivation of land that is highly susceptible to erosion. Some programs and policies actually exacerbate such problems. Price support programs encouraging production invite intensive farming on fragile lands

For these reasons, existing federal programs that promote private land conservation need to be strengthened, and policies that promote non-conserving land use should be reformed. Federal and state laws should be strengthened to reduce nonpoint source pollution from private land. Emerging land management techniques, such as conservation tillage, should be applied in a safe and effective manner. Conventional conservation techniques must be used more effectively to reduce or eliminate pollution, soil erosion, the loss of fish and wildlife habitat, and the degradation of aesthetically valuable open space.

In addition to preventing problems caused by misuse of private land, increasing attention should also be given to protecting private lands that have important natural and cultural values. Relatively new land preservation approaches as well as continued reliance on traditional ones should be pursued more vigorously.

Farm Policy and Natural Resources

Designed during the Depression, the government's farm support programs were intended to protect farmers' incomes and to balance commodity supply and demand. The cost of this intervention in agricultural markets was relatively modest at first, but has since grown exponentially. In 1983, the cost of farm support programs approached a staggering $28 billion.

The rising cost of farm programs along with the environmental implications of certain programs, have led agricultural economists and environmentalists to agree that farm programs need a major overhaul. Certain government policies promote non-conserving use of the land. Depreciation allowances in the tax code, for example, encourage the installation of irrigation systems on land poorly suited to sustained crop production. In addition, some farm price and income supports subsidize the destructive cultivation of highly erodible land.

Responsible stewardship of the nation's agricultural resources is necessary to assure a stable, long-term supply of food and fiber for domestic needs. In the face of fluctuating but generally increasing demand for U.S. farm products, the linkage between commodity production and conservation cannot be ignored. The economic problems of agriculture can be resolved in large part through means that further the interests of conservation and reduce government outlays.

Prime Farmland

Available statistical evidence reveals alarming rates of farmland conversion in the United States. While disagreement surrounds precise numbers, there is strong evidence that prime farmland (that land with the best physical and chemical properties for sustained cultivation) bears a disproportionate share of the total acreage converted from crop production to non-agricultural uses. This fact is disturbing since prime farmland supports most of the nation's crop production for domestic and foreign markets. Prime farmland loss can shift crop production to less productive and more erosive lands. Then, to maintain accustomed yields on these marginal lands, farmers will ultimately require larger investments in fertilizers and pesticides.

Fortunately, interest in prime farmland protection has lately been on the rise in all levels of government. State and local farmland institutions are increasing faster now than ever before. Several federal agencies have adopted policies that address the need to consider farmland protection in policy and program decisions. The Farmland Protection Policy Act, enacted as part of the 1981 farm bill, seeks to minimize the significant contribution of federal programs to the unnecessary loss of the nation's best farmland to non-agricultural uses.

Soil Erosion and Nonpoint Source Pollution

The United States faces significant soil erosion problems. Wind and water remove six billion tons of topsoil from nonfederal lands each year and over one-third of the nation's cropland is eroding at rates that threaten long-range productivity. The Great Plains region today faces circumstances reminiscent of the "dust bowl" days of the 1930s.

The recurring instability of farm income has encouraged farmers to plow fragile land in years of high prices and, in slack years, to sacrifice needed conservation measures in an attempt to avoid financial losses. As farmers increase cultivated acreages, expansion often tends to be on highly erodable lands, resulting in increased soil erosion.

While soil erosion has long been recognized as a threat to productivity, off-site damages are of equivalent concern. Sediment is the most abundant of all United States surface water pollutants, resulting in special costs estimated to be as high as a billion dollars annually, not including significant damage to fisheries. Cultivated land is responsible for at least 40 percent of the sediment load in streams, as well as a high proportion of chemical nutrients and pesticides in runoff. Eroded sediment fills up reservoirs, increases the frequency and seriousness of floods, clogs navigation facilities and canals, interferes with hydraulic equipment, increases the cost of treating drinking water supplies, destroys aquatic wildlife, encourages algae growth, and diminishes recreation potential of downstream waters.

Sediment and chemical pollutants from farms, forests, mines, and city streets constitute a major impediment to the achievement of fishable and swimmable water quality in U.S. waterways. The cost of nonpoint source pollution has been estimated at approximately $6 billion per year. Past government attempts to control nonpoint source pollution have been largely unsuccessful.

Federal soil conservation programs took shape in the early days of the Depression when a prolonged drought dramatized the need for a remedy. The Soil Conservation Service (SCS) was established in 1935 to combat the problem, and, in 1936, additional legislation provided payments to farmers to shift acreage from soil-depleting surplus crops to soil-conserving legumes and grasses. The program was administered by the Agricultural Stabilization and Conservation Service (ASCS).

In 1945, the Agricultural Conservation Program was established to provide farmers direct cash payments to carry out approved soil and water conservation measures. Friction between SCS and ASCS came from competing goals involving production-oriented and conservation-oriented practices. In the 1980s, erosion controls have been further complicated by severe fiscal constraints. Recent inventories of erosion conditions in the United States show that a large portion of erosion occurs on a relatively small number of highly erodible acres. Existing conservation programs cannot protect these lands; new strategies are needed.

Private Forest Lands

Approximately one third of the United States is in forest land, some of which is administered by the U.S. Forest Service. The majority of it, however, is in private hands. To most people the most obvious use of forest lands is timber. However, no less important are other uses including recreation, wildlife habitat, water supply, and rangeland. The importance of the productivity of forest lands is heightened by the anticipated increase in demand for forest products. The U.S. Forest Service has estimated the demand for timber will significantly increase in the next century.

To help reduce the pressure on the national forest system, considerable attention is being given to nonindustrial private forests (NIPF), those where the owners do not have wood processing facilities and the timber is sold to another individual or corporation for processing. It is estimated that less than 50 percent of the nation's timber resources come from NIPF ownerships. Such ownerships, however, provide about 80 percent of the hardwood timber supply. In addition, only about 10 percent of the acres harvested by NIPF owners are being prepared for intensive regeneration or are being harvested in a manner to promote regeneration. Increasing the amount of timber being harvested from these forests is possible. Doing so would reduce pressure on the national forest system. Some provisions in the federal tax code, such as the tax credit for reforestation, promote timber production on nonindustrial and other private forest land. However, other provisions, such as the capital gains treatment, are of questionable benefit and may actually reward those owners who grow a single crop of trees and then convert the land to other uses.

Although the issue of forest land conversion is not nearly as widespread as agricultural land conversion, it is still troublesome. Another concern is the amount of water pollutants coming from forest lands. Unless more stringent and effective pollution controls are adopted, increasing pollution will occur as more private forest lands are cut.

A series of actions should be taken to improve the management and productivity of private forest lands. But given the uncertainty of the needs and desires of private forest land owners, the initial important step should be a study to determine the most effective changes in current laws, programs, and policies to promote wise, efficient management of private forest lands.

Mining on Private Lands

A federal regulatory scheme exists to deal with the environmental problems caused by surface mining for coal on private lands. Under the Surface Mining Control and Reclamation Act of 1977, mandatory national minimum standards were established under a state primacy system for regulating the surface effects of coal mining. In addition, the public was granted rights to participate in all aspects of mining. However, no comparable scheme exists to deal with the problems posed by mining on private lands for other minerals such as copper, molybdenum, sand and gravel, uranium, and phosphates. In a limited number of major mining districts in states such as Colorado, Utah, Arizona, Florida, Minnesota, and Idaho, significant problems in land use, pollution, and long-term care are posed by such mining. These problems are not now addressed on a coordinated, site-oriented basis, for jurisdiction is divided between federal, state, and local authorities.

Loss of Important Landscapes

The vast landscapes of the United States hold a wealth of magnificent natural and cultural areas. Many of these have been protected as part of the national park system or other federal land management programs and by state and local governments. But many other outstanding areas remain largely unprotected and are increasingly threatened by new development. For a variety of political, economic, and other reasons, many of these areas are not likely to be included in any federal protected land system.

An approach that could protect such important areas is establishment of what are commonly referred to as greenline parks. Areas that could be protected in this way are those that tend to be too populous and developed and have too many ongoing economic activities to be considered seriously for inclusion in a federal protected land system.

The greenline approach involves cooperation among various levels of government and the private sector. It differs from management by a federal agency in that relatively little land is acquired, and protection relies to a great degree on state and local land-use regulatory powers. A major intent of this approach is to allow new and existing compatible economic activities, such as agriculture and tourism, to continue and expand, while restricting incompatible development. In addition, new compatible development, possibly including light industry and housing subdivisions, is channeled into the parts of the land-scape best able to withstand the effects of such development.

The greenline approach has been used both in New York's Adirondack Mountains and New Jersey's Pine Barrens. In addition, some elements of the greenline approach can be found in the legislation establishing Lowell National Historical Park, Jean Lafitte National Historical Park and Preserve, and Santa Monica Mountains National Recreation Area.

A related approach is that of ecosystem management areas. The Chesapeake Bay may serve as a model. An innovative combination of protections would affect the bay. It includes expansion of existing wildlife refuges and park areas, designation of an estuarine sanctuary, scenic river designations on the Chesapeake's tributaries, support for the efforts of the Maryland Critical Areas Program that covers most of the Bay's shoreline, and enforcement of pollution control laws. Local, state, and federal governments as well as citizens from several states would be required to cooperate in realizing the goals of the new system.

Local, state, and national conservation land trusts will need to continue and expand their efforts to preserve land through fee acquisition and other approaches. These efforts can be of particular value in greenline parks where government acquisition will be limited. Even with increased efforts, however, there will be a significant need to continue land acquisition funding from the Land and Water Conservation Fund. Private efforts to preserve land must be pursued in addition to government acquisition programs and not as a replacement for those programs.

In addition, efforts should be made by governments and private organizations to educate all citizens regarding the ethical use of land—acceptance of individual responsibility for the health of the land and an understanding of how people are linked to and depend on the land.

Recommendations

Prime Farmland

The Farmland Protection Policy Act established a modest impact assessment process for highways, housing projects, and other federal activities that convert prime farmland; it urges that agencies of the U.S. government at least explore alternatives before undertaking or otherwise subsidizing unnecessary prime farmland conversion. Unfortunately, the U.S. Department of Agriculture has failed to implement the Act in any

meaningful way. Therefore, to advance better agency accountability for United States government programs and actions that
convert prime farmland to non-agricultural uses, the Farmland
Protection Policy Act should be strengthened, and implementation of the Act should be improved.

- **Congress should strengthen, and USDA should better
  implement, existing laws which seek to minimize the
  federal role in the unnecessary and irreversible conversion of the nation's prime farmland.**

Responsible urban growth management is often essential
to the protection of good agricultural land. Successful state and
local initiatives, such as Oregon's land use planning legislation,
should be established elsewhere. State and local jurisdictions
should retain the primary role in farmland protection, but
should be able to draw upon assistance provided by the U.S.
Department of Agriculture.

- **State and local governments should utilize land-use
  planning and growth management to better protect the
  farmland resource.**

Soil Erosion

During times when commodity prices are increasing, farmers are tempted to expand production to marginal lands. Sodbuster sanctions would discourage the plowing of highly erodible lands by denying farmers access to crop price supports,
direct payments, crop insurance, certain farm loan programs,
and other USDA programs. Farmers who convert wetlands important to flood control, waterfowl, and aquatic life should also
be subject to similar sanctions.

- **Congress should enact a strong sodbuster policy that
  would deny USDA program benefits to any farmer who
  plows highly erodible land without taking soil retention
  precautions. Similarly, swampbuster provisions should
  be enacted to deny USDA program benefits to farmers
  who drain, fill, or otherwise convert wetlands to croplands.**

By reducing overproduction caused by overuse of fragile
land, the United States can bring production more closely in line
with demand while eliminating the most damaging soil erosion
and related water quality problems. Highly erodible land now in
cultivation should be retired permanently from intensive row
crop production. A conservation reserve would be a cost effective way to protect topsoil by giving an incentive to farmers to establish and maintain protective cover on reserved land.

- Congress should create a permanent soil conservation reserve that would compensate farmers for converting highly erodible land from row crops to sustainable uses such as wildlife habitat, grass, or trees.

The positive effects of crop rotation on yields, soil nutrients, and pest and weed control have been recognized for centuries. In recent decades, the benefits of rotation have been overlooked as the use of chemical fertilizers and pesticides has increased. Government programs have encouraged this move away from crop rotation by establishing a crop acreage base. By giving more benefits to farmers who have more acreage in production, government programs have contributed to the soil erosion problem. Farmers should be allowed to voluntarily set aside good cropland and plan appropriate rotations without penalty of losing base acreage in the event of a future mandatory acreage set-aside.

- USDA should establish a set of incentives and credits to encourage crop rotations that save soil and reduce surplus crop production.

Mining on Private Lands

Although the Surface Mining Control and Reclamation Act of 1977 (SMCRA) exists to deal with the environmental problems caused by surface mining for coal on private lands, no comparable scheme exists to deal with the problems posed by mining on private lands for other minerals such as copper, molybdenum, and phosphates.

- Congress should enact new legislation such as that recommended in the National Academy of Sciences report on non-coal mining (COSMAR) to provide a focused and coordinated program for districts with non-coal mining on private lands. The legislation should contemplate close cooperation with the states involved. In drafting the legislation, particular attention should be given to SMCRA's national standards, mandatory inspection and enforcement, and public participation provisions.

When mining concludes, many mine sites are abandoned, leaving behind long-term problems such as erosion, subsidence, and significant water quality problems including acid drainage and abandoned tailings, and sedimentation ponds which often contain toxic substances and heavy metals. These and other problems exist on both public and private lands and could adversely affect water supplies for future generations.

- Congress should institute a program of providing perpetual care for abandoned mine sites. The program could be financed through a tax on the products mined.
- Cleanup of abandoned uranium tailings disposal sites should proceed quickly with efforts made to seek reimbursement for federal and state costs from the uranium industry, as provided for under the Uranium Mill Tailings Radiation Control Act. Promulgation and implementation of federal and state regulations for reclamation and disposal of uranium mill tailings at currently licensed sites should proceed without further delay.

Alternative Agriculture Technologies

Contemporary farmers are overly dependent on expensive and environmentally hazardous chemicals, and have inadequate access to information on alternative techniques. Alternative agriculture technologies such as organic farming, multiple cropping, intercropping, and agroforestry should be researched and encouraged to a much greater degree than is now the case. New soil-building crops should also receive attention for the part they may play in increasing diversity and quantity of food and fiber.

- Congress should fund research in alternative farming techniques that conserve soil and water and reduce farmers' dependence on chemical fertilizers and pesticides.

Private Forest Lands

The tax code has a very definite effect on forest management practices. While some provisions are beneficial, others are of questionable value at best. The General Accounting Office, for example, has questioned the argument that capital gains tax treatment results in higher productivity and increased planting.

- Congress should amend the tax code to require those taking capital gains treatment to invest a significant proportion of the savings in reforestation.

Loss of Important Landscapes

Efforts must be continued to preserve significant landscapes that are currently unprotected or inadequately protected. In many cases such areas should be preserved as part of an existing land management system. In other cases, new approaches must be pursued to prevent the loss of important areas.

- Federal, state, and local governments should adopt new preservation techniques, including greenline parks and ecosystem management areas, to ensure the preservation of those valuable natural areas that otherwise will go unprotected.

Protected Land Systems

Protection of natural resources on public lands is an important aspect of this nation's land ethic. Many of the country's most outstanding natural, scenic, and cultural treasures, rugged back country, recreation sites, and wildlife habitats are on lands designated by law as part of specially preserved systems.* Americans are familiar with the national parks, wildlife refuges, wild and scenic rivers, and trails, and with wildlands on the national forests. Units of the National Wilderness Preservation System, which receive still further protection, overlie each of the other systems. In addition, marine plants and wildlife find refuge in protected waters, including estuaries and marine sanctuaries.

---

*The national park system was established in 1916 by an organic act providing for a National Park Service to preserve and interpret nationally significant natural landscapes and ecosystems and the country's historic and cultural heritage. The National Wilderness Preservation System was established by the 1964 Wilderness Act to assure that some land areas are protected in their essentially untouched, natural condition. National wildlife refuges are land units managed first and foremost for wildlife conservation (the system lacks an organic act). The national wild and scenic rivers system was established in 1968 by the Wild and Scenic Rivers Act to preserve unique water resources. National marine sanctuaries were authorized in 1972 under the Marine Research, Protection and Sanctuaries Act to preserve resources of the nation's coastal waters.

Americans have wisely preserved a variety of their resources for the benefit of present and future generations. However, there is considerable need to preserve additional natural areas and to enhance protected land systems. Protected systems need to be expanded, and wise stewardship must be exercised to mitigate threats to resources.

Expansion of protected systems to include new areas worthy of preservation will provide a start. However, even the achievement of designation is fraught with debate over which resources to preserve, how, and when. Trade-offs between protected status and commodity development are likely to be unbalanced if accurate and sufficient resource data are not available to policy makers. Designation of protected land areas can involve costly lawsuits, protracted debates, and needless withdrawals of commodity resources if a sound data base is not an integral part of the planning process.

The Forest Service Roadless Area Review and Evaluation (RARE) program exemplifies the situation. RARE was undertaken to evaluate the resources on roadless national forest lands and to make management recommendations based on the findings. However, inadequate resource information has plagued the program since its inception in 1970, resulting in lawsuits, court injunctions, and a second (RARE II) and third (RARE III) attempt to carry out the needed resource evaluations.

In the forest planning process, enormous amounts of time, effort, and money have been wasted largely because of insufficient data and inattention to adequate environmental protection. There are many other examples ranging from overgrazing on Bureau of Land Management lands to the deterioration of ecologically sensitive soils, wildlife habitat, plant species, and archaeological resources—the result of improper development —where it is clear that lack of resource data created or contributed to significant management problems, some occurring too late to be solved by protective designation.

System expansion in and of itself does not guarantee that proper preservation measures will be taken. Many resources, even within the boundaries of protected systems, are in peril. Both the congressionally-requested 1980 "State of the Parks Report" and a similar 1982 study by the U.S. Fish and Wildlife Service documented thousands of existing and potential threats to parks and refuge resources. The parks report listed more than 4,300 threats, divided almost evenly between external causes and internal conflicts. The Fish and Wildlife Service study reported 7,717 threats affecting more than 22,800 refuge resources; 4,443 of the threats were externally caused, 1,360 conflicts stemmed from internal sources, and 1,914 threats were attributed to both external and internal causes. Parks, wildlife refuges, wilderness areas, forests, and river systems are experiencing air and water pollution. Many are victims of oil spills, leachings from mine tailings, and road construction activities that cause accelerated siltation into streams and lead to destruction of fisheries. Others suffer encroachment by exotic species and overgrazing by domestic livestock.

A major internal management problem is the sometimes negative impact of visitor use. This impact is largely inadvertent; nonetheless, the Fish and Wildlife Service study found that 1,570 threats on refuges resulted from public use, including littering, trampling of vegetation, and wildlife disturbance. The major threat internally for the national parks was overuse. Numerous similar conflicts have been reported on all systems. The situation becomes more urgent in light of a steady growth in the demand for outdoor recreation. The number of visits to national park units illustrate this trend most graphically, increasing from 33 million in 1950 to more than 340 million in 1984. Visitor days in Forest Service wilderness areas alone more than doubled over a 12-year period, from 4.6 million in 1970 to 11.2 million in 1982. Approximately 70 million visitor days were recorded on Bureau of Land Management lands in fiscal 1983.

The conflict caused by Americans loving to death their parks, wildlife refuges, forests, rivers, and trails comprises only one of many headaches for system administrators and managers. They are also faced with conflicts among other uses. While many system "organic" laws require the preservation of resources in their natural state, on-the-ground application is difficult to achieve in light of inadequate budgets for resource data base compilation, visitor carrying capacity studies, and enforcement personnel, among other necessities. The wildlife refuge system actually lacks an organic statute, and thus each new refuge tends to be guided by *ad hoc* principles that may fit one situation but not another. Haying and domestic livestock grazing, for example, may be compatible with wildlife habitat provisions on a particular refuge. Yet, in practice, these activities usually disadvantage wildlife.

On the poorly inventoried Bureau of Land Management lands, resources that need proper assessment to determine their ultimate designation include scientific, scenic, recreational, ecological, wildlife, historical, and archaeological values as well as soil, rangeland, and water. The Bureau is directed by law (the

1976 Federal Land Policy and Management Act) to study its lands for their wilderness potential and report recommendations for wilderness to the President by 1991. The relatively haphazard process now under way to determine which values on these lands should be protected is continually challenged by development interests, even when specific commodity supplies are readily available elsewhere.

Recognizing the constraints imposed on resource preservation by special interest groups, bureaucratic mechanisms, competition for funding sources, and other factors, it is necessary to outline the steps needed to bring the land ethic to full fruition on protected public land systems. The problems can be solved through a combination of careful advance planning and adequate human and financial resources to carry out those tasks that will ensure proper preservation of a national savings account consisting of some of the nation's most special natural, cultural, and historic treasures. Future generations should be left a heritage on which they can build an enriching life.

Recommendations

Resource Protection

Among the wide array of challenges facing protection of valuable natural and cultural resources, expansion of the major protected land systems is currently the most pressing issue, and is likely to remain so in the years ahead. Lands that qualify are needed for preserving overall ecosystem integrity as well as diversity, but continuing development pressures will soon cause many areas to lose their special natural qualities. The primary goal is to ensure that suitable portions of all basic ecosystems are preserved in federal protected land systems through carefully considered additions to the national park, wilderness preservation, wildlife refuge, and wild and scenic rivers systems. Protection is also important for the qualifying estuaries, marine areas, and trails through inclusion in their respective protected categories.

National Parks

The goal is to continue building on the distinctive contribution of America's national parks to the nation and the world.

- **Congress should enact long-pending proposals for new parks, and the national park system should be rounded out to completion in accordance with the National Park System Plan.**

- The National Park Service should undertake a vigorous land acquisition program to secure or protect private inholdings needed for completing existing park units, and Congress should support this action by making adequate annual appropriations from funds available in the Land and Water Conservation Fund.

National Wilderness Areas

One goal is to add enough areas to represent and preserve the diversity of the country's natural resource base, ensuring that suitable and adequate portions of each of the nation's 232 basic ecosystems are included in the National Wilderness Preservation System. All the remaining roadless lands in the national parks, wildlife refuges, and forests and on Bureau of Land Management lands should be reviewed periodically for their suitability to be added to the System, to preserve as much of the remaining wildlands as possible.

- Congress should designate suitable areas to be included in the National Wilderness Preservation System. Alternatives to wilderness designation should not be accepted. Agencies responsible for managing the various federally protected land systems should seek to acquire suitable nonfederal lands for wilderness designation.

National Wildlife Refuges

While recognizing the importance of other systems in protecting wildlife, the vital role of the national wildlife refuges in preserving fish and wildlife should not be underplayed. The goal is to provide prime habitat areas for each vertebrate species (game and nongame) and its ecosystem native to American soil, waterways, and coastal regions.

- As with National Park Service units, Congress should acquire land to complete existing refuge units and new areas containing critical wetland and upland habitat.

National Wild and Scenic Rivers

The national wild and scenic rivers offer significant potential for ecosystem protection. Expansion of this still fledgling system is essential to watershed quality and recreation opportunities in particular, and in several instances to the preservation of fish, wildlife, and plant species. In a 1982 inventory that covered all of the states except Alaska and Montana, the Interior Department identified 1,500 rivers and river segments as eligible for the system.

- Congress should add to the national wild and scenic rivers system suitable rivers and river segments identified as eligible for the system. Of the 3.5 million river miles in the U.S., a reasonable goal is the protection of two percent—or 70,000 miles—of the most outstanding rivers by the year 2000.
- States lacking wild and scenic river programs should establish such programs, and Congress should provide incentives and assistance.

Marine Sanctuaries and Estuaries

Special contributions offered by marine sanctuaries and the nation's estuaries to marine wildlife and plant preservation need to be maintained.

- Congress, acting on state and federal agency recommendations, should enlarge the marine sanctuary system by designating areas already qualified by the National Oceanic and Atmospheric Administration (NOAA) for inclusion. Forty new areas currently targeted by NOAA for designation should be added over the next 20 years.
- Congressional oversight is needed to ensure that the management of marine sanctuaries and estuaries is strengthened.

Acquisition Funding

Necessary expansion of protected federal land systems and preservation of their valuable resources will require substantial expenditure of federal dollars for acquisition. Opportunities for suitable land purchases are rapidly diminishing because of expanding development and resulting higher land prices.

- To enable the federal government to meet this challenge better, Congress should enact legislation providing that the unappropriated balance in the Land and Water Conservation Fund be converted to a trust fund that would generate interest revenue. (The Fund is authorized to receive $900 million annually from various sources including Outer Continental Shelf royalties. Congress has yet to appropriate the total $900 million in any fiscal year.)

Zones of Influence

While expansion of protected land systems protects resources, specific steps are also needed to protect existing systems from threats posed by activity outside their boundaries. A priority consideration is the need to alleviate such threats as a proposed coal strip mining project only a few miles from spectacular Yovimpa Point in Bryce Canyon National Park; the possibility of locating the nation's first high-level nuclear waste dump in Davis Canyon on the border of Canyonlands National Park; and air pollution caused by nearby coal-fired plant and coal mining activities that is adversely affecting several national parks, refuges, and forests in the West.

- **Congress should enact legislation requiring all protected land system managing agencies to establish "zones of influence" for their respective units, based on an ecosystem approach. The legislation should require that any federal activity or any activity on federal land adjacent to a protected land system unit be consistent with protection of the unit's resources, and should also require the elimination of all federal subsidies or incentives to development within the zones, similar to provisions in the recent Barrier Islands legislation. Once such legislation has been enacted, the relevant federal agencies should work with all concerned individuals and entities in a regional context to develop mutually agreeable protection plans within the zones.**

Internal Conflicts

Given the number and variety of internal conflicts currently experienced on protected land systems, a series of actions is necessary both to ensure a healthy resource base and to enhance the visitor's experience.

- **Federal agencies managing protected lands should conduct baseline data studies and complete resource protection plans on all protected systems units; review generic and individual designation statutes that allow development or consumptive use of system resources and make recommendations to Congress for resolving conflicts; and produce and implement visitor carrying capacity studies for all protected land systems and their individual units. The federal government should undertake greater support of the efforts of the states to provide outdoor recreation and cultural preservation for their residents. State lands, reserved for recreation and cultural appreciation, offer the opportunity to help meet the demand for recreation, serving also to alleviate visitation pressure on the major federal land systems.**

Institutional Aspects

Many of the previous recommendations for protected land systems constitute ideas already on the drawing board, resulting in part from mandates already issued but not fulfilled, or are logical extensions of policy now in place. Shifts in human resources, budget and management priorities, and policy objectives will be necessary to attain the goals. However, there are several actions, of what may be called an institutional nature, that will require the commitment of new philosophy and resources but which are important to the future of the country's protected land systems.

National Wildlife Refuges—Organic Law

In assessing specific inadequacies in protected land system administration, one glaring omission cannot be overlooked—lack of an organic law for the national wildlife refuges. Currently, the refuges are under the jurisdiction of the U.S. Fish and Wildlife Service's Refuge Division with little but the dictates of agency policy manuals to guide its overall supervision.

- Congress should provide an organic act that identifies the wildlife refuge system's purpose, lists criteria for planning and management, and grants it stronger and more consistent protection. The following policy statement might serve as the basis for the act:

    The policy of the U.S. Fish and Wildlife Service shall be to consolidate the protection, acquisition, and management of the nation's prime wildlife habitat, including forests, rangelands, tundra, deserts, wetland and upland habitats, and waters, into the national wildlife refuge system; provide for the protection, enhancement, and restoration of vertebrate species, including endangered and threatened species, on such refuges; uphold the nation's commitment under international agreements and treaties relating to wildlife conservation; and provide that any public use and enjoyment of these resources be consistent with and contribute to this policy.

Resource Inventories

To achieve protected land system expansion in a desirable fashion and to protect natural and cultural resources on those systems, detailed resource inventories are essential.

- The Department of the Interior should establish a multi-disciplinary task force to analyze existing natural and cultural resources inventory programs carried out by protected land system managing agencies. Appointees would include representatives from federal land managing agencies as well as from public interest groups concerned with public land management and from appropriate research institutions. Making use of existing data from a variety of sources such as the U.S. Geological Survey, the Nature Conservancy's Heritage Program, federal land managing agencies, and university research centers, the task force should identify weaknesses in the information gathering and analytical techniques of managing agencies and then work with responsible individuals or institutions to propose measures intended to correct uncovered shortcomings. A major goal of the task force should be to assess the existing federal land managing agencies' inventory programs with an eye toward determining how effective they are in fulfilling policy objectives, including review of federal land systems for potential wilderness areas and the preparation of resource management plans. The task force should concentrate on the sufficiency of inventory programs as they relate to various ecosystems within the major physical/climatic regions of the country, rather than as they relate to arbitrary boundaries such as state lines.
- Congress should establish zones of protection for qualifying Bureau of Land Management lands that are not now of wilderness character but that contain significant natural, historic, scenic, scientific, and wildlife values.

Internal Management

One of the major needs of federal protected systems is to strengthen internal management and administration of protected units within the systems.

- Management plans for all system units should be produced and updated no less than every ten years; designation of additional wilderness should be reviewed; concessioners should be limited to the operation of appropriate commercial facilities; and close cooperation between various protected land managing agencies should be encouraged on issues such as devising sound methods for conducting resource inventories.

Building a Constituency

All major environmental issues require a solution at the local, state, national, or international level. Essential to meaningful protection of major land systems is a large, informed, and active constituency that supports protective status for significant natural and cultural resources. Government entities, while not the proper mechanism for fostering political activism, nevertheless have a role to play in educating the public on the value of the nation's protected resources.

- All federal land managing agencies' interpretation programs should focus more attention on the principal features of each system unit and the relative importance of those features as examples of a specific eco-type within a larger environment or landscape or of a time or place in history or pre-history. Increased cooperation should occur between educational entities and groups such as the National Association for Environmental Education to provide quality environmental education curricula in the public schools.
- Citizen organizations should work to improve their ability to increase public understanding of critical natural and cultural resource matters.

Public Lands

The nation's public lands comprise one-third of the land in the United States and three-quarters of all the territory under U.S. jurisdiction, when seabeds in the exclusive economic zone are included.

Interest in the management of the nation's public lands has grown over the last 20 years as pressures on the public domain have intensified. While the agencies managing these lands have given greater attention to environmental values in their planning in recent years and that planning has become more sophisticated, at the same time political pressures upon these agencies from commodity interests have become intense and more overt. The managing agencies are less and less able to solve problems themselves. This, in turn, leads to the need for more and more intervention by Congress.

In contrast to the earlier focus on the opportunity for nature reserves on these public lands, citizens today are truly concerned about the future of these lands as a whole. Their interest is in emphasizing the need for sound, long-term management of the nation's public resources.

Five Goals

Five central goals are reflected in the 20 key recommendations presented here. The first is to institute planning which will ensure truly balanced multiple use of public lands. Too often in the past, management of these lands has overwhelmingly emphasized production of commodities such as timber, minerals, oil, or grazing, while conservation values have been recognized only in those places that have little commodity interest. Recommendations that deal with timber sales in national forests, lowland trails, grazing, coal leasing, and mining operations on both national forest and Bureau of Land Management (BLM) lands, and Outer Continental Shelf oil and gas leasing arise from a need to build more legal checks and balances against excessive exploitation of the nation's public lands.

A second goal is to bring more economic rationality into the exploitation process. The use of better and more comprehensive tools of economic analysis is especially necessary in the management of public resources. Fees and sale prices should reflect fair market value, and these equitable payments can then be reinvested in rehabilitating degraded lands. Commercial forest land classification should reflect a finding that timber can be grown profitably, non-fuel minerals on public lands should not be given away, and uneconomic land holding patterns should not be perpetuated.

A third goal is to protect areas with special natural values. While larger areas are protected under existing systems, other areas possessing special natural values should be protected by management restrictions. These could include areas with old-growth timber, riparian habitat, soil-hazard areas, Areas of Critical Environmental Concern, small natural areas, areas unsuitable for mining, sensitive seabed and coastal areas, and wilderness areas where mining claims should be eliminated.

A fourth goal is to bring about new regulatory programs for major mining operations dealing with minerals besides coal and for disposal of mining refuse that poses long-term threats.

A fifth and final goal is to address many long-neglected problems such as reformation of the Mining Act of 1872 and improving the protection of environmental values under the Mineral Leasing Act of 1920, as amended. Publicly owned mineral resources continue to be given away, with public land managers having little control over how and where hardrock mining takes place. In addition, old claims in Forest Service wilderness areas and in other key areas should be weeded out now that the

20-year dispensation for filing additional mining claims has expired. Also, improvement is needed on many BLM rangelands now in poor condition.

Another need is to correct the century-old problem of checkerboard landholdings in the national forests brought about by railroad land allotments. Access to such national forest lands is sometimes blocked, making them difficult to manage. Also, the job of completing land acquisition for national forests in the East should have a high priority.

Recommendations

Forest Lands—National Forest

While National Forest land is classified according to whether it is suitable for sustained yield timber production, some lands may not be able to grow successive crops of timber at a profit. Such timber is cut at a loss and produces uneconomic sales, particularly when administrative costs are considered.

- To correct this problem, the Forest Service should prepare benefit-cost studies which would classify such lands according to those which can be operated with a favorable benefit-cost ratio. Lands where costs exceed benefits, and where timbering adversely affects environmental values, should be removed from the long-term commercial forest land base.

In certain circumstances the Forest Service may sell more timber from a national forest unit in a given decade than the forest unit can produce in succeeding decades. This practice, known as "departure from sustained yield," violates the sound practice of conserving the timber resource.

- Congress should repeal the "departure from sustained yield" provision and adhere to a policy providing for a non-declining, even flow of timber from the national forests.

Being a small percentage of the nation's forest base, the national forests should provide values and products that cannot or will not be produced from private lands. Congress recognized this role in the National Forest Management Act by requiring that the natural diversity of plant and animal species be preserved in the national forests. A vital and essential element of ecological diversity is the retention of a well distributed representative system of old-growth forests.

- Congress should specify that an adequate portion of the remaining old growth on each national forest, between 15 percent and 25 percent, be retained in order to assure that the diverse fish and wildlife, scientific, recreational, and other related values that such forests provide are protected.

Abused Lands

Millions of acres of public lands stretching from Alaska to Arizona have been overgrazed or damaged by irresponsible mineral exploration and development, logging, or intensive recreational use. Lax implementation and inadequate funding of the present conservation programs have been major stumbling blocks to correcting the problem.

- Congress should establish an earmarked fund to rehabilitate public lands suffering from abuse and neglect. Funds for this purpose should come from a surcharge on the fees paid by the users who have created the problems (e.g., grazing fees, mineral royalties, stumpage fees). In addition, the royalty fees paid on Outer Continental Shelf (OCS) leases should be adjusted to better reflect a fair return to the public (using royalty rates being levied by states for comparison), with the added revenues being put into a trust fund. The interest earned annually on these revenues should be added to this rehabilitation fund. Rehabilitation targets should be established for every state having such problems, and annual progress reports should be issued.

Recreation

In the last 15 years, use of off-road vehicles, including snowmobiles, dune buggies, motorbikes, jeeps, and motorcycles on federal lands has proliferated. When used in sensitive or inappropriate areas, ORVs have inhibited other recreational uses, destroyed cultural and archaeological resources, and interfered with livestock grazing and other multiple uses. Two executive orders have been issued—the first by President Richard Nixon in 1971 and the second by President Jimmy Carter in 1977—requiring that the land management agencies minimize impacts from ORVs by closing unsuitable lands in order to prevent resource damage. The agencies, however, especially BLM, have implemented these orders unevenly and have allowed much incompatible ORV use.

- Congress should pass legislation establishing standards for the prevention of adverse environmental effects from ORV use. The statute should direct agencies to shift ORV use toward areas less susceptible to damage.

In its recreation planning under the Resources Planning Act, the Forest Service puts too much emphasis on quantitative factors such as user days and number of improved recreational sites, and gives too little weight to maintaining the landscape and the quality of the experience.

- The Chief of the Forest Service should direct national forest planners to weigh qualitative factors equally with quantitative factors.

Large percentages of the national forest trail system are being lost to logging operations and roads, which intrude on most of the timbered country. In mountainous terrain, most low-elevation trails that are usable in the winter have been obliterated or lost.

- Congress should require the Forest Service to prepare new plans and then reconstruct a trail system through lowland holdings in national forests, and protect these trailside corridors from logging.

Watershed Management

Current Forest Service and Bureau of Land Management watershed management practices are fragmented, rarely taking account of the cumulative effects of the agencies' activities throughout a watershed. Neither the totality of the impacts of any one activity on a watershed (all timber harvesting planned for a watershed over a decade) nor the interplay of various management activities within the watershed (logging, grazing, mining, and recreation) are systematically analyzed by the agencies.

- The Forest Service and the Bureau of Land Management should prepare up-to-date soil hazard maps to enable them to assess comprehensively the cumulative impacts of planned activities. These steps will provide a basis for sound watershed management plans.

Management

Under present law the BLM is authorized and directed to establish Areas of Critical Environmental Concern (ACECs) on its lands as an outgrowth of its planning processes. It is an oversight that no such provisions exist with respect to the national forests nor for other public land administration systems such as the Tennessee Valley Authority (TVA), military reservations, or Outer Continental Shelf lands.

- Congress should authorize and direct the Forest Service and managers of TVA, military reservations, and Outer Continental Shelf lands to establish Areas of Critical Environmental Concern. Citizens should be enabled to petition the administering agencies to designate given ACECs, and thereupon the agencies would be required to make various investigations and findings and to do so within a designated time.

Federal agencies have generally done an inadequate job of identifying and designating unique natural areas on their holdings which are worthy of special protection (Areas of Critical Environmental Concern, outstanding natural areas, research natural areas, etc.). As a result, dozens of national natural treasures are being threatened by leasing, mineral development, off-road vehicle abuse, and other incompatible uses.

- Congress should direct federal land management agencies to work with states to establish interagency councils to review the adequacy of existing natural area programs and to set targets for further protection. These councils would be composed of representatives of all the federal land management agencies operating in the state, a representative of the governor, and a representative of any independent organizations whose primary purpose is the identification of unique natural areas.

The federal government has not adequately prosecuted those who violate pollution laws, and does not impose fines that provide credible deterrents. However, many of those firms which violate pollution and other environmental laws also desire to buy federal natural resources.

- Congress should enact legislation which provides that those who violate federal environmental laws on a recurrent and serious basis are disqualified from bidding on federal land sales and leases of natural resources (timber, coal, oil, gas, geothermal, etc.). Such legislation would provide a strong incentive for complying with pollution laws.

Acquisition of Land

Barely half of the lands authorized for acquisition within the boundaries of eastern national forests have yet been acquired. The presence of large private holdings in these forests causes problems in terms of public access and adverse development.

- Congress should develop a program of sustained funding to enable the Forest Service to purchase additional private lands within the boundaries of every national forest by the end of the century. The goal is to achieve Forest Service management over 50 to 75 percent of the forest area. In some cases, acquisitions could be arranged through a more flexible exchange process with private owners, or could involve purchase of less than the full ownership rights as long as environmental values are protected.

Checkerboard land ownership patterns resulting from railroad land grants have in certain cases seriously hindered public access on large amounts of national forest land in the West and made it difficult to manage intermingled public lands.

- Congress should ask the Office of Technology Assessment (OTA) to study various effective ways of expeditiously combining these checkerboard patterns into larger, consolidated units, including earmarking revenues from sales of "excess" federal property for this purpose.

Mining and Drilling

The 1872 Location Mining Act is obsolete, gives away public resources, affords little discretion to managing agencies, and includes no protection for the environment.

- Congress should replace the 1872 Location Mining Act with a modern law which vests administering agencies with discretion to determine where and under what conditions mining will be allowed. The new law also should require protection for environmental values, adjust mining operations to maximize compatibility with other land uses, take commodity needs into account, and secure fair-market value for the public under leasing arrangements (as opposed to either claims or patents). The new law should also require rehabilitation of mined sites and require that unpatented claims under the 1872 Act be converted to leases within a specified period.

While the Mineral Leasing Act of 1920 reserves more authority to protect the public interest than the 1872 law, in practice this authority is too rarely applied. Blanket leasing of oil and gas over large areas of the public domain often engulfs strategic parcels of key wildlife habitat, fragile watersheds, and scenic beauty. Protecting these non-mineral values is difficult once the pressure of a vested private property interest in the underlying minerals has been created.

- The Mineral Leasing Act of 1920 should be amended to require thorough consideration of and compatibility with wildlife, recreation, and other environmental values in decisions as to whether to issue leases, and on the administration of drilling and production activity once leases have been granted.
- The administration should issue clear directions to surface managing agencies to consider the no-lease alternative on sensitive areas and not feel compelled to lease regardless of potential consequences.
- Decisions regarding on-shore mineral leasing should be adminstratively delegated (under existing law) to the agency with immediate responsibility for the surface resources of an area so that consideration of all resources can be integrated in mineral management and not fragmented, as now occurs.

Many mining claims that have been filed on public lands are legally deficient because they have been abandoned, were not recorded under the Federal Land Policy Management Act of 1976 (FLPMA), or failed to have the required annual assessment work done.

- The Forest Service should aggressively pursue legal procedures to invalidate such claims, particularly in wilderness areas and other environmentally sensitive lands. Moreover, Congress should enact new legislation earmarking a portion of funds derived from federal mineral leasing to acquire valid claims in such areas. Congress should also require that all holders of mining claims within wilderness areas prove the validity of their claims within five years and all claims not validated should be extinguished.

The federal government owns the mineral estate on vast holdings where it long ago sold the surface rights. Under the Surface Mine Reclamation Act provisions for coal, it can only lease the underlying coal when the surface owner consents.

- Congress should extend the Surface Mine Reclamation Act provisions for coal to require the consent of the surface owner in the case of other minerals as well, particularly when extraction produces surface disturbances, such as with phosphate mining.

Outer Continental Shelf Development

The present Outer Continental Shelf (OCS) oil/gas and mineral leasing program is based on a decision-making process which lacks basic data and information necessary to make intelligent choices as to which areas should be offered. Under current modeling procedures, the Department of the Interior has rarely identified an area as being too sensitive to be leased because of more important environmental values. This has often led to battles between states and the federal government over leasing of areas which turn out to have minimal petroleum or mineral development potential.

- **Congress should provide the National Oceanic and Atmospheric Administration with adequate funds to sponsor research, collect known information, and identify and map those areas with particular biological and environmental values and geologic hazards as well as those areas which have commercial value for mineral mining and oil and gas. Also, the Secretary of the Interior should delete from development plans those areas with high biological values or geologic hazards, especially where commercial potential is low. Where conflicts could still occur, the Secretary should assure that development is undertaken at a sufficiently measured pace to minimize risks to the living resources.**

Conflict frequently occurs in the OCS leasing program between the federal government and state and local governments. Recent court decisions have greatly impaired what was already a limited ability on the part of the states to seek redress in the OCS oil and gas leasing program. Congress in its original legislation anticipated a state-federal partnership with a built-in consultative process.

- **Congress should reaffirm that oil leasing plans of the Department of the Interior be consistent with state coastal management programs.**

Coal Leasing

As with the Outer Continental Shelf program, indiscriminate leasing of coal and other energy minerals can result in significant environmental damage, as well as financial losses for taxpayers. Over the course of the last four years, the federal coal program has come under a great deal of scrutiny for the way it has sought to lease large quantities of coal without regard to the actual need for more coal leasing to meet energy demand, or to the environmental consequences of mining in particular areas of the American West.

The General Accounting Office has estimated that the government received $100 million less than fair market value from public coal auctions held in 1982. David Linowes, chairman of a special commission appointed in 1983 to look at the coal program and fair market value, pronounced the leasing program "deficient in all of its functions." The congressional Office of Technology Assessment (OTA) in a 1983-84 study observed shortcomings in the Department of the Interior's land use planning process.

OTA noted that previous pauses in the coal leasing program had been ended with expectation that leasing decisions would in the future be based on comprehensive planning and environmental impact assessment, leases would be developed in a timely manner, and the public would receive a fair return on publicly owned lands. These remain, however, the biggest problem areas in federal coal leasing today. Reform legislation passed in the 1970s, including the Federal Land Policy and Management Act (FLPMA), intended that public lands be managed for a number of purposes, of which energy development is only one.

- **The Department of the Interior should identify lands suitable for leasing rather than have industry nominations drive the planning process. Areas of Critical Environmental Concern should be deleted at the beginning of the leasing process and significant resources such as water, wildlife, and other natural values should be protected. The Department should not hold new coal sales until it can show that the coal is needed for the purpose of meeting reasonable forecasts of energy demand, and that it has finished an environmental impact statement and the regional resource management plans required by the Federal Land Policy and Management Act.**

In 65 years of federal coal leasing, less than one billion tons of the 18 billion tons of coal leased has been developed. The coal industry in 1983 (the last year for which figures are available) was producing each year only .006 of the coal it currently holds under lease from the government. One requirement of coal leasing reform legislation enacted in 1976 was that companies must turn back any new leases they obtain if, after a period of 10 years, there has not been "diligent development" of the lease (defined as one percent annual production of recoverable reserves).

A second requirement was that after 1986, any company not relinquishing its non-producing, pre-1976 leases would be barred from obtaining new mineral leases of any kind.

- **Congress should resist any effort to weaken diligent development provisions in present law.**

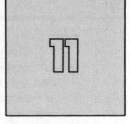

Urban Environment

More than 70 million people live today in America's metro-politan areas. Millions more reside nearby and frequently depend on cities for employment, shopping, culture, and enter-tainment. A majority of the nation's 500 largest corporations are headquartered in urban America, as are the bulk of the banking, financial, government, and educational institutions.

The next two decades hold difficult challenges for the na-tion's urban centers, especially in relation to public health and environmental quality. In addition to poverty and social equity issues, the inner cities face serious air and water quality and solid waste dilemmas as well as unmet open space, recreation, and land use needs. Advances on these fronts must complement progress on urban social issues if the quality of life is to be im-proved for city residents and the environmental benefits cities offer to the nation as a whole are to be preserved.

Air Quality

Emissions from motor vehicles and nearby industrial sources, combined with concentrated living patterns and, in some cases, meteorological conditions that trap pollutants are among the factors that have caused urban areas traditionally to record the nation's worst air quality. Despite modest improvements over the last decade in levels of some traditional pollutants, significant urban air quality problems remain. Violations of national health standards for carbon monoxide and ozone, increasing nitrogen oxide levels, toxic air pollutants, millions of tons of sulfur oxide emissions, and indoor air pollution characterize air quality in and over much of urban America. Also, motor vehicle emissions continue to pose health hazards.

Diesel Emissions. Although the Environmental Protection Agency has established emission standards for all vehicles, diesel emissions from motor vehicles will still pose a significant pollution problem for urban areas. Uncontrolled diesels emit roughly 30 to 100 times more particulates than existing gas-powered engines. These fine particulate emissions can elude the body's defenses and penetrate deeply into the lungs. The particulates are coated with known and suspected carcinogens, mutagenic materials, and other toxic substances. Diesel particulates also degrade urban visibility.

Solving the diesel problem should become a top-priority air quality issue for the nation's urban areas. City traffic already includes the heaviest concentration of buses, almost all of which are equipped with diesel engines. New truck purchases are shifting dramatically from gasoline to diesel power. The National Research Council of the National Academy of Sciences projected in 1981 that by the year 2000, virtually all trucks and 25 percent of automobiles will run on diesel fuel. Industry analysts say that despite recent declines in purchases of diesel autos, there will unquestionably be long-term growth in sales of these vehicles, and that they will occupy a substantial share of the U.S. market by the end of the decade.

Indoor Air Pollution. "Because most people spend more than 80 percent of their time indoors," warns the 14th Annual Report of the Council on Environmental Quality (1983), "the potential health effects of indoor air pollution may be more serious than those resulting from outdoor air pollution." Indoor air pollution takes many forms: gaseous products from unvented indoor combustion, tobacco smoke, radioactive gas from subsoil or well water, toxic chemicals from cleaning agents, disinfectants, or pesticides, formaldehyde, and asbestos, as well as other pollutants, viruses, and bacteria. Many of these substances have been linked to cancer, heart, and respiratory diseases, infectious diseases, and allergies.

The multifaceted indoor air quality problem is nationwide in scope, but is of special concern to cities for two reasons. First, urban dwellers generally spend more of their time indoors than suburban or rural people. Second, city residents are more likely to rent, rather than own, their apartments or homes; as a result, they have less control over building and insulation materials and ventilation systems used in their homes.

Indoor air pollution could become increasingly serious in the future. Stepped-up weatherization and insulation of homes and offices are much needed conservation measures. But care must be taken so that such strategies do not contribute to a buildup of indoor air pollutant concentrations, especially in buildings without adequate air circulating systems. Unfortunately, the growing use of synthetic chemicals in home construction and furnishings is likely to compound the indoor air quality problem.

Drinking Water

The nation's urban drinking water systems differ in many ways, because the cities they serve vary in size, topography, climate, hydrology, and social and political settings. But urban water systems share similar problems of potentially enormous magnitude—threats of contamination from toxic pollutants and nonpoint source runoff, as well as uncertainty surrounding their ability to satisfy future water demand.

Protecting the Source of Urban Water Systems. The magnitude of the toxic pollution problem in urban water supplies is largely unknown, but the risks of serious contamination are growing. Thirty-five percent of the nation's cities rely on underground sources for their drinking water needs. EPA has located roughly 180,000 surface impoundments containing liquid wastes and 90,000 industrial and municipal landfills containing solid wastes. Many of these waste sites are not secure and pose potential threats to underground water systems. These sites are scattered around the nation, but are concentrated in the heavily populated regions of the country.

Urban water systems that draw upon surface waters must contend with runoff from discrete point sources as well as the more elusive problems of non-point source runoff from agriculture and enroaching development in watershed areas.

Urban Drinking Water Supply and Demand. Over the next two decades, the nation's cities will face growing difficulties in supplying enough water to meet the need. Residential water use in metropolitan areas alone will increase by 31 percent, according to the U.S. Geological Survey.

Urban water supply problems fall into two main categories. Older cities in the Northeast and Midwest face major infrastructure repair and maintenance problems. Many have postponed rehabilitation of their aging systems and are plagued by leaking pipes and tunnels. Cities have reported losing from 10 percent to more than 30 percent of their total water through inadequacies in their infrastructure network. The other category of problems affects cities in the more arid regions of the country which have developed faster than the ability of government to meet water needs.

Garbage Disposal

Nearly every metropolitan area in the country is facing a serious garbage disposal problem or will be in that position over the next two decades. Americans produce 150 million tons of garbage annually. This figure is expected to increase to 225 million tons per year by 1990. Over the last few decades, cities have disposed of the bulk of their trash in landfills. This practice, however, has produced well-known environmental and public health problems. Cities are quickly running out of landfill space, and suburban and rural communities are becoming increasingly reluctant to provide landfill space for wastes from other jurisdictions.

In an effort to find disposal alternatives, some localities have recently turned to garbage incineration, sometimes called resource recovery. This process burns garbage and, as a by-product, produces electric power. There are now about 50 such garbage-burning facilities operating around the nation. By the end of the century, this number could grow to several hundred, with adequate financial support and environmental safeguards.

The emerging shift to large-scale garbage-burning as the preferred disposal method raises potentially serious environmental consequences. The primary threat is to air quality. Uncontrolled incinerators emit large amounts of acid gases, toxic metals such as lead, and hazardous organic compounds including dioxin. To date, the record of these facilities has been mixed, and several plants have been shut down as a result of uncertainties surrounding air emissions. One EPA survey of several facilities showed organic emissions to vary widely. Aggressive federal and local controls are necessary to assure that threats to groundwater from landfilling are not replaced by toxic air quality risks posed by large-scale garbage-burning.

Urban Sprawl

The nation has witnessed an unprecedented shift of population, jobs, and development from the inner cities to suburban areas and beyond over the past 25 years. This trend has had major adverse environmental consequences. Leap-frogging development has gobbled up millions of acres of prime agricultural and recreational lands. Sprawled building and living patterns have significantly increased energy consumption. And poorly planned development has threatened water supplies and resources.

These trends have been fostered in large measure by legislative policies and government subsidies. Financial aid for highway construction, sewage treatment grants for growth in outlying areas, and other rural development assistance programs have all been catalysts for unplanned or poorly planned sprawl. Government decision-makers must now eliminate these wasteful subsidies and adopt land use policies that are compatible with wise stewardship of the nation's land resources.

Public Transportation

The country's public transit systems are facing a myriad of complex problems. While management and productivity issues require additional attention, transit funding will remain a central issue facing urban decision-makers. Older transit systems have long been starved for funds; many have had to reduce critical maintenance and repair services. Newer systems, meanwhile, have found it difficult to secure monies to initiate or complete construction. The Congressional Budget Office has estimated that the nation's public transit systems will require an investment of $65 to $99 billion ($3.6 - $5.5 billion a year) between now and the year 2000 for rehabilitation and new capital investment. Significantly smaller sums are presently available, and relatively little of today's transit funding comes as the predictable, multi-year grants so critical to long-range transit planning.

Urban Recreation

Unless remedied by direct government intervention, inadequate recreation opportunities will continue to erode the quality of life for the nation's urban residents over the next two decades. The problem is one that has traditionally beset inner cities. As with other urban infrastructure problems, the deterioration of outdoor and indoor recreational facilities has in some cases actually accelerated in recent years. Demand for recreation in cities is increasing, however, and the loss of existing and potential urban recreational land, facilities, and programs is becoming a matter of great concern in urban America.

The recreational needs of urban residents are diverse. Inner city youngsters should have the opportunity to visit large, open parks and be introduced to the wilderness experience. They also need expanded urban parks, playgrounds, and athletic fields closer to home. Such opportunities must be easily accessible since many urban dwellers are without automobiles and unable to travel long distances to satisfy their recreational needs. Reinvestment in existing recreation facilities, conversion of existing urban space into recreation space, and initiation of creative programs to enhance recreation and the attractiveness of cities must be included in the overall solution.

The federal government has an important role to play in this effort. From 1978-1984, the Urban Parks and Recreation Recovery Program (UPARR) provided planning, development, and innovative program grants to city groups who were rehabilitating existing facilities and initiating new recreation programs. UPARR, which funded nearly 500 project grants and over 300 planning grants for the most distressed and recreation-poor cities and counties, was a cost-efficient approach and one of the few government programs attacking these issues. It now faces extinction due to budget cuts.

Recommendations

A renewed commitment to America's cities is needed in the 1990s and beyond. Key long-term priorities are clean air, safe drinking water, effective disposal of garbage, control of urban sprawl, and improving of public transportation and recreation.

Air Quality

Pollution in urban areas where millions of people live and work still exceeds national health standards for such widespread air contaminants as carbon monoxide and ozone (photochemical smog), although in some areas progress is being made. Nitrogen oxides, however, are expected to increase further during the next decade. The millions of tons of sulfur oxides that are emitted annually, primarily from power plants and other industrial sources, will continue to cause environmental havoc in the form of acid precipitation. New government initiatives must be implemented if the Clean Air Act promise of healthful air quality in the nation's urban areas is to be fulfilled in this decade. Also, given the large number of persons affected, the potential for significant visibility loss and the likelihood of continuing increases in vehicle emissions, new regulations are needed.

- Congress, in amending the Clean Air Act, should retain strict requirements for health-based national ambient air quality standards and incorporate acid rain provisions that would reduce sulfur oxide and nitrogen oxide emissions.
- EPA should tighten its standard for automotive diesel particulates; issue more stringent standards for particulate and nitrogen oxide emissions for diesel trucks and buses; investigate the possibilities for using alternative fuels to power diesel engines; and initiate a vigorous program of in-use inspections and recalls for vehicles with defective pollution control equipment.
- The Consumer Product Safety Commission, in coordination with EPA, should, under existing statutory authority, begin regulating carcinogenic and other toxic products commonly found in building materials and home furnishings.
- HUD, in consultation with EPA, should develop a model building code with provisions that would limit the use of dangerous substances in building construction and provide ventilation design guidelines to prevent the build-up of harmful indoor air contaminants.

Drinking Water

Many urban water systems are threatened with contamination from toxic pollutants and many face uncertainties as to their abilities to assure adequate water supplies. Of the 90,000 industrial and municipal landfills and 180,000 surface impoundments containing liquid wastes, it is not known precisely how many pose potential threats to the 35 percent of the nation's cities which rely on underground sources to meet their daily water needs. Older cities face major infrastructure and repair problems, while newer cities have developed so rapidly that local governments have not been able to meet the growing needs for water. Many cities have overbuilt sewage and water supply capability, thus encouraging urban sprawl.

- EPA should establish strict nationwide standards for toxic drinking water contaminants; strengthen ground water protection by tightly regulating the underground injection of industrial waste, the underground storage of toxic chemicals, and the application of pesticides in areas above aquifers; and accelerate its review of permit discharge limits and examine the effects of such discharges on drinking water quality.

- State and local governments should adopt stringent controls on land development and pesticide use in watershed areas to mitigate the impact of non-point pollution on surface drinking water supplies.
- States and localities should adopt stringent urban water conservation plans with tax incentives for retrofitting of inefficient water appliances and fixtures in existing buildings; revise water rate structures to eliminate or reduce discounts for bulk users; and phase in universal metering of residential water use.

Garbage Disposal

Most urban areas are facing a serious garbage disposal problem, or will be during the next 10 to 20 years. As an alternative to landfills, which pose environmental and public health risks, some urban areas are now disposing of garbage by incineration. But the shift toward large-scale garbage burning raises potentially serious environmental consequences of its own. Accordingly, government officials must exercise special caution in dealing with this complex technology.

- EPA should enforce stringent emissions limitations for garbage-burning incinerators by tightening its new source performance standards for such facilities (the existing California Air Resources Board guidelines are a model to consider) and by revising these standards as improvements in this swiftly-changing technology are developed.
- EPA should encourage emerging technologies for solid waste disposal, closely monitor new technological developments, and issue technical guidance on a regular basis to guide states and cities in selecting disposal and incineration programs that provide maximum assurances of public health protection.
- State and local governments should commit to implementing solid waste reduction measures as a means of conserving resources and allowing municipalities to build smaller, or perhaps fewer, garbage-burning incinerators (state legislation should mandate that cities de-

velop recycling strategies as part of their overall waste management program).
- States should require, as a condition for granting incinerator operating permits, that localities make siting decisions to minimize public exposure to incinerator emissions, install equipment for the comprehensive and continuous monitoring of furnace operating conditions and air emissions, and provide for automatic furnace shutdowns, if monitoring reveals that emissions standards or design specifications are exceeded.

Urban Sprawl

As population, jobs, and development have moved from the inner cities to suburban and exurban areas over the past 25 years, housing and industrial development have impacted on prime farmland and recreational lands, increased the consumption of energy, and threatened water supplies and resources. To a significant extent, these trends have been fostered by legislative policies and government subsidies.
- Congress and the Executive Branch should recognize the interrelation between federal actions and urban impacts, and eliminate tax breaks, investments, grants, and loans for programs that encourage scattered development of open countryside.
- Congress should establish a Select Committee on Urban Affairs to provide a focus for reformulating national urban policy over the coming decades.
- States should establish land use programs that preserve agricultural and recreational areas, and adopt policies that encourage urban and suburban in-filling and cluster building in place of haphazard siting of new development.
- States should adopt strategies for urban decentralization, including taxing and investment policies that support urban objectives and downtown redevelopment.

Public Transportation

The failure to resolve the public transit crisis threatens to create major problems in urban America. There are currently 125 million cars operating in the United States. These vehicles consume the equivalent of 6.6 million barrels of oil per day, or about 1.6 million barrels more than the nation imports. The Office of Technology Assessment projects that by the year 2000, there will be 56 percent more cars on the road than there were in

1975; the number of total trips, mostly in and around cities, will increase by 75 percent. But building new highways in urban areas is physically impractical and environmentally unsound. Roadway congestion, travel time, and gasoline consumption will increase and harmful motor vehicle air pollutants will remain at unacceptable levels unless public transit systems—the lifelines of urban America—receive priority government attention over the next two decades.

- Congress should increase the motor vehicle gasoline tax (one cent of which now goes into a transit fund for capital projects) at least five cents a gallon for the next 15 years, with the extra revenues going into the transit capital fund. Each one cent increase in the gasoline tax will raise $1 billion per year.
- Congress should maintain federal operating subsidies and seek to restore this program at least to 1980 funding levels.
- States and localities should provide stable sources for transit operating assistance by enacting legislation to generate funds from a selection of broad-based regional taxes.

Recreation

A critical shortage of recreation lands, facilities, and programs is having a profoundly adverse impact on the quality of life in urban America. Although demand for recreation in cities is increasing, existing opportunities are often inadequate and in many cases deteriorating. All levels of government should be doing more to address these basic needs.

- Congress should enact legislation providing that the unappropriated balance in the Land and Water Conservation Fund be converted to a trust fund that would generate interest revenue, and should authorize that significantly higher levels of appropriations be allocated to states so as to address more adequately urban open space and recreation needs. (Note similar recommendation in Protected Lands chapter.)
- Congress should continue adequate appropriations for both the Urban Parks and Recreation Recovery Program and the Land and Water Conservation Fund, with monies from the latter source being used for open space acquisition and new facility development both outside urban areas and in inner cities.

- Congress should enact and the President should sign legislation creating a national conservation corps whose young men and women would undertake diverse recreation, environmental, and community improvement projects.
- State and local governments should also establish conservation corps programs and take other actions to improve park and recreation services such as facilitating the shared use of existing physical resources among schools, community groups and individuals, and assisting in the establishment of local organizations to participate in "adopt-a-park" programs.

International Responsibilities

The Global Connection

When an oil spill tarnishes a beach, a wilderness area is invaded by mineral extraction or logging, or a city's soil and water is contaminated, local people usually act quickly to counter the environmental abuse. But with environmental catastrophes far distant from their community, people feel there is not much they can do. Yet what happens in other parts of the world can, and often does, affect the United States. Consider the following examples:

Panama. Passage through the Panama canal, important to U.S. and world trade and vital to U.S. national security, is severely limited during the dry season by lack of depth capacity in Lake Gatun. This low water level results from excessive logging for firewood by growing numbers of landless farmers on the hillsides surrounding the canal (the population of Panama has grown from 300,000 at the turn of the century to more than 2 million today). U.S. military forces based in Panama did not take action to address the environmental deterioration. Now the U.S. Agency for International Development (AID) has spent $18 million for reforestation and watershed management programs, and is planning to spend $2.2 million in 1985.

Haiti. Forests in Haiti began to disappear 25 years ago because they were being cut beyond their capacity to regenerate.

As population increased (Haiti's population growth is among the highest in Latin America and its poverty level is the worst), Haitians have cut 80 percent of the timber from the hillsides, exposing fragile topsoil to tropical rains which quickly wash it into the sea. The intense sun has baked the land, eliminating its porosity so that the ground can no longer absorb rainwater and restore groundwater aquifers. The soil cannot support adequate agricultural production. This loss of both food and water sources has driven Haitians to abandon their land. What appeared initially to be a Haitian problem has thus become a domestic U.S. problem as these tragic environmental conditions have forced Haitians to seek refuge in Florida.

Madagascar. A large island where natural processes have long been free from excessive human intervention, Madagascar has in recent years lost 90 percent of its forests and 70 percent of its vegetation. Nine of the original 30 lemur species are extinct, five are endangered, and 12 are threatened. An increase in population from one million in 1900 to nine million today has led to widespread poverty as food, firewood, and housing needs claim 40 to 50 square miles of forest each year. Efforts to increase agricultural production have failed. In 1970 Madagascar signed a $35 million World Bank loan agreement for a project to irrigate 29,000 acres around Lake Alaotra, with the expectation that it would triple the area's rice production in ten years. Five years after completion of the project, an independent evaluation team from the Bank concluded that the project had made "no significant contribution" to the economy of Madagascar. The report revealed a lack of Bank expertise in natural resource management and a failure to take into account the traditions and social needs of the people.

Pesticides Export. Under federal law American manufacturers of pesticides that have been cancelled or not approved for use in the United States are free to export them. Large quantities of some 40 such pesticides are still being shipped to more than 50 other nations. These exported pesticides are often used on cash crops that in turn are shipped back to the United States and other industrialized countries. Nearly half of the imported green coffee beans tested by the Food and Drug Administration in 1978 contained measurable levels of pesticides that had been banned for most uses in the United States. Freshly cut flowers brought in from Colombia caused poisoning of American florists. Overuse of pesticides in Central America has led to high levels of pesticide residues in produce and beef destined for the United States. The U.S. Food and Drug Administration's testing for illegal pesticide residue levels in the more than $13 billion worth of food imports each year is inadequate, allowing foreign and U.S. consumers and workers to be exposed to the dangerous pesticides.

Atmospheric Carbon Dioxide. Between 1958 and 1983, carbon dioxide in the atmosphere increased nine percent, primarily due to emissions from the burning of fossil fuels as well as burning of forests and crop residues. Scientists estimate that a doubling of atmospheric carbon dioxide levels would heat the global atmosphere by an average of three degrees centigrade, with substantially greater increases at the poles. This warming could affect rainfall patterns and agricultural production and could cause some melting of the ice caps of Greenland and the Antarctic, raising ocean levels and drowning coastal cities around the world. The United States, which uses 25 percent of global commercial energy, is a major contibutor to the problem. Some scientists fear the effects could also result in climate changes that could cause significant reductions in U.S. grain production.

The Antarctic. The Antarctic continent, the only land mass that is part of the global commons, is presently in its relatively pristine state and is the last great wilderness in the world. It is of prime importance to global climatic and weather systems, and provides key nutrients to the rest of the world's oceans. It is the home of two-thirds of the world's seals, furnishes the basic food supply for over a million whales each year, including several species that are gravely endangered, and is the breeding area for over 80 million penguins and many millions of other sea birds.

Sixteen countries, including the United States, are presently carrying out the Antarctica Treaty of 1959. But the next few years could hold severe dangers for the continent. Its potential oil and mineral wealth have received wide attention, both from multinational development corporations and the Third World countries which do not want to be excluded from any profits that may accrue. Antarctic krill, a shrimp-like animal which potentially constitutes the world's largest marine food resource, is being heavily fished by the Soviet Union and Japan. Blue and humpback whale populations, once common in the Southern Ocean, have been harvested into commercial extinction by whaling fleets. Although disasters from energy and mineral development or proven over-harvesting of Antarctic krill have not yet been recorded, Antarctica remains a fragile ecosystem exceedingly vulnerable to destruction if not protected.

Regional Seas. International relations and regional stability can, on the other hand, be enhanced through efforts to solve environmental problems that cross national boundaries. In fact, negotiations on environmental matters sometimes may be the only contact between two countries. When the Mediterranean Sea became threatened with pollution, even long-standing enemies were willing to cooperate to save this shared natural resource. Countries with traditionally strained relations—France and Algeria, Egypt and Israel, Spain and Morocco, Italy and Tunisia, Greece and Turkey—are all participants in the United Nations Environment Programme's Mediterranean Action Plan. By 1982, 10 Regional Seas programs embraced 120 countries. The United States has been negotiating to take part in both the Caribbean program, which includes Nicaragua and Cuba, and the South Pacific program. Draft protocols for oil spill situations and ocean dumping are part of the two programs. Conclusion of the South Pacific treaty will require the United States to consent to a protocol prohibiting radioactive dumping. At present the United States opposes such a protocol even though it has no plans for any U.S. radioactive dumping in the area.

Nuclear War. A threat that surpasses all of the rest is that of nuclear war and its long. term impact on planet-wide climate and biological support systems. As noted in the Nuclear Issues chapter, scientific findings disclosed at the 1983 Conference on the World after Nuclear War, and since then substantiated by a National Academy of Sciences study, showed that even a limited nuclear war could produce sub-freezing temperatures and darkness over the earth for months. This so-called nuclear winter could lead to the extinction of species, the collapse of ecosystems, and the possible destruction of civilization as it is now known.

Population Growth. Another overriding global problem that impacts on all of the other issues is human population growth. As discussed in the Human Population Growth chapter, world population is nearing five billion, and the human species is beginning to consume the productive resource base of the planet. In many countries, the land cannot support the additional people. Worldwide population growth has many impacts on the United States, such as stresses on soils in the effort to meet increasing demands for food, or pressure on American forests to meet world needs, and large numbers of people emigrating to the U.S., adding greatly to U.S. population pressures.

National Security

These examples illustrate that destruction of the natural environment as a result of population growth, poverty, industrial demands, and inappropriate development affect not only the countries where the problems occur, but are of acute concern to the United States, affecting national security, the economy, and the environment. The examples indicate that decisions which are driven by short-term gains that fail to protect the natural resource base often lead to human and economic disruptions which destabilize peoples and governments. Economic distress, degradation of environmental quality, and displacement of peoples will—if multiplied in many countries throughout the world—confront the United States and all countries with a precarious future.

U.S. national security is increasingly dependent on the prosperity and stability of developing nations. Environmental stress can be a significant factor in destabilizing these and other countries. When this happens, as in Central America, the costs to the United States can be enormous. The Kissinger Commission report calling for an $8 billion "Marshall Plan" to Central America, failed to address environmental issues and gave minimal attention to the underlying problem of excessive population growth. It is long past time for a redefinition of national security to include this important dimension.

Economic Welfare

As indicated by the examples of Haiti and Madagascar, environmental stress can inflict on developing nations an endless cycle of poverty. If this occurs widely in the developing world it will have serious adverse effects on the economic future of the United States. Developing countries already buy 35 percent of U.S. exports and account for 37 percent of U.S imports. When a Brazil or a Mexico cannot pay its debts, the United States feels the impact. Projections indicate that developing nations will produce an increasing share of global wealth, and future U.S. economic growth may well depend on finding major markets there. Similarly, the Haiti example illustrates that environmental stress can cause large numbers of people to flee their native land and seek refuge in the United States. Illegal immigrants from neighboring nations in the Caribbean and Latin America are adding an estimated one million or more people a year to the population of the United States. Together with legal immigration, this immigration policy has produced a large net population increase in recent years, despite lowered U.S. birth rates. The result is that the United States now has one of the fastest-growing populations among the industrial nations of the world.

Global Ecological Impacts

The buildup of atmospheric carbon dioxide, the exploitation of marine fisheries, and the risk of cataclysmic nuclear war all indicate that the United States is vulnerable to disruptions in life support systems elsewhere in the world. These problems can only be addressed in cooperation with other nations.

Direct or indirect impacts on the United States from environmental stress in foreign nations are not the only reason for concern by U.S. citizens. As Americans become increasingly aware of the plight of those who live elsewhere, deeply held moral values will motivate citizens to seek solutions for the problems of others who share the planet. Although recent years have seen a turning inward and a disenchantment with some of the past efforts to help others, Americans will in the long run be dissatisfied with a world in which hundreds of millions live in misery.

International Development Aid

The United States is the major contributor to the World Bank, the Inter-American Development Bank, and other multilateral development banks. Unfortunately, in far too many instances the resettlement schemes, hydroelectric dams, and agricultural projects of these banks have produced disastrous social, health, and environmental impacts rather than improving conditions for the least advantaged. These impacts include destruction of tropical forests, salinization of productive land, elimination of fisheries, transmission of malaria, schistosomiasis, and river blindness, extermination of species, and loss of areas of great scientific and educational value. For example, in the World Bank's scheme to resettle part of Brazil's population in the northwestern province of Rondonia, pristine tropical forests have been ravaged, planned agricultural development has collapsed because soils are not suitable, and armed conflicts have broken out between the settlers and indigenous Indian tribes whose preserves are being infringed upon.

The multilateral development banks could play a significant role in promoting sustainable development, but the types of projects they implement must change dramatically. The World Bank spends less than one percent of its budget on such vital human needs as nutrition, health, and family planning. Instead of promoting adverse environmental and social impacts, the banks could launch major efforts to restore ravaged watersheds and denuded forests, and could carry out energy efficiency improvements which would benefit all sectors of the economy.

Global Foresight

The most serious limitation in the United States' capability to address international issues of the future is the nearly total lack of any holistic, inter-related, long-term approach to decision-making. Events of the past decade have substantiated the conclusion of the 1980 Global 2000 Report to the President that the executive agencies of the U.S. government are not now capable of presenting the President with internally consistent projections of world trends for the next two decades. And nothing has happened since 1980 to improve the situation.

The energy shortage of the early 1970s, the OPEC oil price increase, the Third World debt crisis, and the African famine all were predictable, yet the U.S. government belatedly realized their implications and was unprepared to deal with them.

An urgent need exists for the President and Congress to establish within the Executive Office of the President a mechanism for bringing the long-range trends in population, environment, natural resources, and development to the attention of policy-makers long before they reach crisis proportions. The federal government should begin immediately to gather needed data and information from all agencies and the private sector, coordinate and analyze them systematically to see their long-term impacts, and present alternative courses of action to decision-makers in time to take preventive measures.

Vital U.S. Role

The United States controls one-fourth of the world's wealth and a greater percentage of its scientific and technical know-how. U.S. leadership in addressing environmental problems, both national and international, has been demonstrated and must continue. The practice of organizing large and influential non-governmental, grass-roots organizations originated in the United States, and has now spread to many other countries. Worldwide environmental, population, natural resource, and development issues are linked with U.S. self-interest and continue to present citizens with the challenge of helping humanity by solving rather than aggravating global environmental problems. The U.S. response during the next few decades will help determine the shape of the human future. The challenge can be met. The history of the U.S. environmental movement demonstrates that cooperation and effort can change adverse trends. But it will require commitment and leadership from U.S. citizens and public officials.

Recommendations

The overall goal must be for the United States to use its influence on the scale that is needed if solutions to the most pressing global issues are to be found. The following recommendations are in addition to those listed elsewhere concerning stabilization of population growth, prevention of nuclear war and nuclear winter, control of hazardous pollution caused by nuclear weapons production and disposal of nuclear wastes, and promotion of energy sustainability.

Funding for AID and Multilateral Banks

Funding requests by the U.S government and authorizations and appropriations by the Congress do not adequately address the problems of global sustainability of resources and stabilization of human populations.

- **Congressional appropriations for the U.S. Agency for International Development and the multilateral development banks should be contingent upon the willingness of these institutions to shift their development priorities into environmental restoration projects that ensure sustainable resource use such as reforestation, watershed restoration, population stabilization, improved energy efficiency, small-scale agricultural projects, and protection of critical ecosystems.**

Funding of International Agencies

Programs and activities of the United Nations Environment Programme (UNEP), the United Nations Fund for Population Activities (UNFPA), the United Nations Food and Agriculture Organization (FAO), the World Heritage Fund, and the Man and the Biosphere Program (MAB) are severely hampered by the inconsistency and uncertainty of contributions from the U.S. government. From fiscal 1980 to 1984, for instance, the U.S. government contributed no funds at all to the World Heritage program although the United States had been the leader in proposing the World Heritage covenant as a means of giving added recognition and protection to unique natural and cultural national parks and historic sites throughout the world.

- **The U.S Government should regularly fulfill its financial obligations to the continuing programs of UNEP, UNFPA, FAO, MAB, and the World Heritage Fund.**

Foresight Capability

Executive agencies of the U.S. government are incapable of presenting the President or the Congress with consistent projections of world trends in natural resource consumption, population growth, environmental consequences of proposed development, or the interactions of these forces. The government is thus unprepared to choose rationally among long-range policies to achieve a more desirable future or to propose and select alternative courses that could prevent potential catastrophes.

- **The Administration should cooperate with the Congress to establish a capacity within the Executive Office of the President to analyze the long-term interactions of population, resources, environment, and development and to provide information relevant to current policy decisions and responsive to the needs of the national and global future.**

Biological Diversity

Species diversity is being lost throughout the world, primarily due to habitat being lost to development and the pressures of expanded population. U.S. AID, in consultation with government resource agencies and non-governmental organizations, has developed a strategy to conserve biological diversity worldwide.

- **Congress should strengthen the AID biological diversity strategy proposal that would coordinate and maximize the effective use of federal funds to preserve a diversity of species throughout the world, and Congress should authorize and appropriate sufficient funds to implement the priority recommendations of the strategy.**

International Trade in Hazardous Chemicals

Shipment of hazardous pesticides and other chemicals to developing countries, even those substances cancelled or unregistered for use in the United States, is not controlled, nor are adequate safeguards in place to regulate U.S. companies in their overseas manufacturing or siting of plants, as evidenced by the Bhopal disaster. EPA is required only to send the receiving country notices of pesticide cancellation actions and notices of the first shipment each year of unregistered pesticides, and there is a similar requirement for other hazardous chemicals. But these limited notices do not even precede the shipment, and no acknowledgment is required to show that they were received by a competent authority.

- Congress should enact legislation modifying the Federal Insecticide, Fungicide, and Rodenticide Act and the Toxic Substances Control Act to require giving importing countries and parties adequate notification of the arrival of hazardous chemicals, to supply information on those banned for use in the United States, and to require the informed consent of importing parties prior to export of such hazardous substances.
- Congress should pass legislation to require that U.S. companies operating abroad adhere to U.S. environmental, health, and worker safety standards.
- Congress should establish a technical assistance program to help developing nations regulate and manage specific facilities utilizing hazardous chemicals exported from the U.S or operated by U.S companies.

Law of the Sea Treaty

As the community of nations looks increasingly to the world's oceans as a source of important raw resources, from fisheries to minerals, it is imperative that any development of these resources be carried out under an umbrella of international law and regulation. Without such law, industrialization and exploitation of ocean resources will take place in a state of anarchy, with the inevitable result of depletion and ruin of the ocean biosphere.

The United Nations has declared that the seas and the ocean bed beyond the 200 mile limits of nations are the "common heritage of mankind" and are not the exclusive realm of any nation, thus are not to be exploited to the disadvantage of others. The UN Law of the Sea Treaty regulates virtually all uses of the oceans, with specific sections on the conduct of seabed mining, sustained-yield fisheries management, pollution control, and other sections pertaining to the environmental health of the oceans. Unfortunately, the Administration chose in 1981 to withdraw from implementing the Treaty provisions, and is currently attempting to operate outside the Treaty regime.

- **The U.S. government should ratify the Law of the Sea Treaty.**

Ocean Dumping

Ocean disposal of radioactive wastes and incineration of hazardous wastes at sea, plus increasing reliance on the oceans for the disposal of other land generated wastes, have been the subject of growing concern around the world. Some of those wastes are extremely dangerous pollutants of the marine environment, and much still needs to be learned about the risks of such dumping. Scientific studies suggest that the accumulation of many of those substances in the oceans can lead to severe ecological repercussions in species and biological processes, and that the substances could be hazardous to human health through foodchain contamination.

- **Department of State and EPA officials, as key representatives to the London Dumping Convention, should encourage and support environmentally sound measures regarding ocean disposal of radioactive wastes, incineration of wastes at sea, and dumping of other land-generated wastes. They should support banning of low level radioactive waste dumping unless its proponents can prove that such activities are safe. Seabed burial of high-level radioactive wastes, which is the subject of ongoing research, should be treated as dumping under the London Convention, and therefore prohibited, unless it is proved that such disposal is technically feasible and environmentally acceptable. Incineration of wastes should be examined much more closely under the Convention, including a comprehensive scientific assessment of the need for such disposal, its risks to the marine environment, and the adequacy of the technology. United States positions in regional forums should be consistent with those taken in the London Convention.**
- **EPA and NOAA should give increased attention to the environmental risks associated with ocean dumping.**

Antarctica

The Antarctic continent's remoteness has been its protection, but it is now threatened on several fronts. The 16 consultative nations participating in the Antarctica Treaty are now considering establishment of a regime to govern both commercial exploration and exploitation of mineral resources on the continent and in surrounding waters. The Soviet Union and Japan are going forward with commercial krill fishing without a sound scientific understanding of the interrelationships of the living resources in the Southern Ocean. The treaty parties have not yet commissioned a comprehensive study to identify appropriate natural areas to be given permanent protection.

- The 16 Antarctic consultative parties should take steps to create an Antarctic protection agency, which would assure that fishing is managed on a scientific basis that does not jeopardize any endangered species. The agency should prepare a comprehensive management plan and conservation strategy for the region which would set aside large protected areas as parks or reserves, and establish sanctuaries to protect the feeding areas of endangered whales.

- The consultative parties should declare a long-term moratorium on all mineral activities in order to allow careful consideration of the best use of Antarctica, including study of the option of protecting the entire continent and its surrounding oceans.

World Conservation Strategy

The World Conservation Strategy was drawn up by the International Union for Conservation of Nature and Natural Resources, the United Nations Environment Programme, and the World Wildlife Fund to help advance the achievement of sustainable development in all nations through conservation of living resources and by integrating conservation and development. The Strategy looks to government policy-makers, conservation groups, and individuals concerned with living resources, and development agencies, industry, and trade unions for achieving the goals. Thirty-three countries have prepared or are preparing national conservation strategies, although the United States is not yet among these nations.

- Congress should endorse the World Conservation Strategy as an overall guide for U.S. actions to conserve biological diversity and direct that all U.S. agencies involved in conserving biological diversity in developing nations cooperate with appropriate international organizations, both governmental and non-governmental.

Conclusion

If focused and directed, the sense of purpose and human potential that all people share will be adequate to persuade decision-makers to correct the serious resource, population, environmental, and development conditions that affect the world. Only through understanding these global issues and giving them their necessary place on the scale of priorities can citizens improve opportunities for sustainable human progress and preservation of the earth's environment.

Bibliography

Background and Synopsis of the Issues

Environmental Quality. Report of the Council on Environmental Quality, 1978.

The Macroeconomic Impact of Federal Pollution Control Programs: 1981 Assessment. Prepared for the U.S. Environmental Protection Agency by Data Resources Incorporated, 1981.

State of the Environment, 1982. Report by the Conservation Foundation, Washington, D.C.

Gallup Poll on Environment. George Gallup, Jr., Princeton, N.J., September 1984.

Nuclear Issues

Report to the Congress as Required by Section 170-P of the Atomic Energy Act as Amended. U.S. Department of Energy, August 1, 1983.

The Cold and the Dark: The World After Nuclear War, The report of the Conference on the Long-term Worldwide Biological Consequences of Nuclear War. Ehrlich, Paul R.; Sagan, Carl; Kennedy, Donald; Roberts, Walter Orr. W. W. Norton, New York, 1984.

The Effects on the Atmosphere of a Major Nuclear Exchange. Committee on the Atmospheric Effects of Nuclear Explosions, Commission on Physical Sciences, Mathematics, and Resources, National Research Council. National Academy Press, Washington, D.C., 1985.

Report to the President by the Interagency Review Group on Nuclear Waste Management, March 1979.

Report on Accidental Release of Tritium Gas at the Savannah River Plant. South Carolina Department of Health and Environmental Control, Division of Radiological Health, May 2, 1974.

Memorandum from G. Halstad to G. Smithwick, October 29, 1982. U.S. Department of Energy, Savannah River Plant Operations.

Lawless, W. F. The Dupont Management of Savannah River Plant Radioactive Wastes. A report to the U.S. House of Representatives Committee on Energy and Commerce, Subcommittee on Oversight and Investigations, November 27, 1984.

U.S. Department of Energy Epidemiological Project Summary for Oak Ridge Associated Universities and the University of North Carolina. U.S. Department of Energy, Office of Health and Environmental Research, Washington, D.C., May 1984.

Arkin, W., Cohran, T., and Hoenig, M. U.S. Nuclear Forces and Capabilities. The Nuclear Weapons Databook, Vol. 1. Ballinger Press, 1984.

Human Population Growth

1985 World Population Data Sheet. Population Reference Bureau, Washington, D.C.

Gupte, Pranay. The Crowded Earth. W. W. Norton, New York, 1984.

The Population Debate: Dimensions & Perspectives. Papers of the World Population Conference, Bucharest, 1974.

Demographic Indicators of Countries, Estimates and Projections as Assessed in 1980. Population Reference Bureau, Washington, D.C.

McNamara, Robert, President, World Bank. Address to the Board of Governors, Belgrade, Yugoslavia, October 2, 1979.

Brown, Lester. Building a Sustainable Society. W. W. Norton, New York, 1981.

State of the World, 1984, a Worldwatch Institute Report on Progress Toward a Sustainable Society. W. W. Norton, New York, 1983.

Caldwell, Lynton K. Population and Environment: Inseparable Policy Issues. The Environmental Fund, March 1985.

Energy Strategies

The National Energy Policy Plan. Report to Congress required by Title VIII of the Department of Energy Organic Act. U.S. Department of Energy, Washington, D.C., October 1983.

A Perspective on Electric Utility Capacity Planning. A report by the Congressional Research Service for the Subcommittee on Energy Conservation and Power, U.S. House of Representatives, August 1983. Committee Print 98-M, 98th Congress, 1st Session.

Gibbons, John, and Chandler, William U. Energy: The Constant Revolution. Plenum Press, New York, 1981.

Chandler, William U. Energy Productivity: Key to Environmental Protection and Economic Progress. Worldwatch Paper 64. Worldwatch Institute, Washington, D.C., 1985.

Vererber, Rudy R. and Rubinstein, Francis M. New Lighting Technologies, Their Status and Impacts on Power Densities. Doing Better, An Agenda for the Second Decade, Volume E. American Council for an Energy Efficient Economy, Washington, D.C., 1984.

Sant, Roger W., Bakke, Dennis W., Naill, Roger F. Creating Abundance, America's Least-Cost Energy Strategy. McGraw-Hill Co., New York, 1984.

Ross, Mark H. and Williams, Robert H. Our Energy: Regaining Control, a Strategy for Economic Revival Through Redesign in Energy Use. McGraw-Hill Co., New York, 1981.

The Road to Trillion Dollar Energy Savings: A Safe Energy Platform. Public Citizen, June 1984.

Audubon Energy Plan. National Audubon Society, New York, 1984.

Water Resources

The Nation's Water Resources 1975-2000, Vol. III, Appendix II. Water Resources Council, Washington, D.C., 1984.

State of the Environment, 1984. A report by The Conservation Foundation, Washington, D.C.

Bowland, John J. Water/Wastewater Pricing and Financial Practices in the United States. Technical Report 1-NMI, 1983. U.S. Agency for International Development.

Maintaining Integrity in Aging Systems, Boston's Approach. Journal of the American Water Works Association, November 1982.

Blackwelder, Brent and Carlson, Peter. Survey of Water Conservation Programs in the Fifty States. A report prepared for the Department of the Interior, Bureau of Reclamation. Environmental Policy Institute, Washington, D.C., August 1982.

Frederick, Kenneth D. Water Supplies. A chapter in Current Issues in National Resource Policy. Portney, Paul R., editor. Resources for the Future, Washington, D.C., 1982.

Current Cost Sharing and Financing Policies for Federal and State Water Resources Development. Congress of the United States, Congressional Budget Office, 1983.

Wetlands of the United States: Current Status and Recent Trends, National Wetlands Inventory. Department of the Interior, National Wildlife Service, March 1983.

Wetlands: Their Use and Regulation. U.S. Congress, Office of Technology Assessment, OTA 0-206, March 1984.

Toxics and Pollution Control

The Clean Air Act. A report prepared for Members of Congress by National Clean Air Coalition, Washington, D.C., February 1983.

State of the Environment, An Assessment at Mid-Decade. The Conservation Foundation, Washington, D.C., 1984.

Report by the Association of State and Interstate Water Pollution Control Administrators in Collaboration with the Environmental Protection Agency, Washington, D.C., 1985.

National Survey of Hazardous Waste Generators and Treatment, Storage and Disposal Facilities Regulated Under RCRA in 1981. Environmental Protection Agency, Office of Solid Waste, April 1983.

Monthly Permit Status Report, Environmental Protection Agency, Office of Solid Waste, April 1985.

Gordon, Wendy. A Citizen's Handbook on Groundwater Protection. Natural Resources Defense Council, New York, 1984.

Lash, Jonathan; Gillman, Katherine; and Sheridan, David. A Season of Spoils. Pantheon Books, New York, 1984.

The Nature and Magnitude of the Air Toxics Problem in the United States (Draft). Environmental Protection Agency, September 1984.

Can We Delay A Greenhouse Warming? A report of the Environmental Protection Agency, September 1983.

Trace Gases Amplify Greenhouse Effect. New Scientist, May 16, 1985.

Environmental Safety. A report of the Environmental Protection Agency, February 1985.

Toxicity Testing Strategies to Determine Needs and Priorities. National Academy of Sciences, 1984.

Wild Living Resources

Smithsonian Institution Report on Endangered and Threatened Plant Species of the United States. H.R. Doc. No. 94-51, 94th Congress, 1st Session (1975).

Convention Concerning the Conservation of Migratory Birds and their Environment, United States-U.S.S.R., November 19, 1976. 29 U.S.T. 4,647.

Endangered Species Technical Bulletin, Vol. 10, No. 4. Department of the Interior, Fish and Wildlife Service, April 1985.

Endangered Means There's Still Time. Fish and Wildlife Service, U.S. Dept. of the Interior, 1981.

Servheen, Christopher. Status of the Grizzly Bear in the Lower 48 States, Progress Toward Recovery. Proceedings of the Sixth International Conference on Bear Research and Management, 1983.

Private Lands and Agriculture

Economic Report of the President, transmitted to the Congress with the Annual Report of the Council of Economic Advisors, February 1983.

National Agricultural Lands Study, Final Report. Council on Environmental Quality, U.S. Department of Agriculture, et al., 1981.

Basic Statistics, U.S. Soil Conservation Service, 1977 National Resources Inventory, December 1982. Statistical Bulletin Number 686.

Sampson, R. Neil. Farmland or Wasteland: A Time to Choose. Rodale Press, Emmaus, PA. 1981.

Soil and Water Resources Conservation Act (RCS): 1980 Appraisal, Part I. U.S. Department of Agriculture, March 1981.

Rasmussen, Wayne D.. History of Soil Conservation, Institutions, and Incentives. From Soil Policies, Institutions, and Incentives. Halcrow, Harold, et al., editors. Soil Conservation Society of America, 1982.

Clark, Edwin H., II; Havercamp, Jennifer; and Chapman, William. Eroding Soils: The Off Farm Impacts. The Conservation Foundation, Washington, D.C., 1985.

Paarlberg, Don. Farm and Food Policy: Issues of the 1980s. University of Nebraska Press, 1980.

Soil Conservation in America: What Do We Have to Lose? American Farmland Trust, Washington, D.C., 1984.

An Analysis of the Timber Situation in the United States, 1952-2030. U.S. Department of Agriculture, 1982.

The Federal Role in the Conservation and Management of Private Nonindustrial Forest Lands. U.S. Department of Agriculture, 1978.

Forest Productivity Report, Forest Industries Council. National Forest Products Association, Washington, D.C., 1980.

Protected Land Systems

Fish and Wildlife Service Resource Problems: National Wildlife Refuges, National Fish Hatcheries, Research Centers (Draft). Department of the Interior, U.S. Fish and Wildlife Service, August 1982.

State of the Parks. Report to the Congress. Department of the Interior, National Park Service, 1980.

Department of the Interior and Related Agencies Bill, 1984 Report. H.R. Doc. No. 98-253, June 2, 1983, 98th Congress, 1st Session.

National Inventory of Rivers. Department of the Interior, 1982.

Public Lands

The Exclusive Economic Zone Papers, Oceans '84 Conference. National Oceanographic and Atmospheric Administration, September 1984.

Fifty Years of Public Land Management. Department of the Interior, 1984.

Land Areas of the National Forest System. Department of Agriculture, U.S. Forest Service, September 1984.

Sect. of the Interior v. California 104 S.Ct. 656 (Jan. 11, 1984).

Analysis of the Powder River Basin Coal Lease Sale. General Accounting Office, May 11, 1983.

Environmental Protection in the Coal Lease Program, Congressional Office of Technology Assessment, May 1984.

Federal Coal Leasing Amendments Act of 1976. Public Law 94-377.

Urban Environment

Environmental Quality 1983. Annual report of the Council on Environmental Quality, Executive Office of the President, 1984.

Diesel Cars: Benefits, Risks and Public Policy. National Research Council. National Academy Press, 1982.

Gordon, Wendy. A Citizen's Handbook on Groundwater Protection. Natural Resources Defense Council, New York, 1984.

Rebuilding America's Vital Public Facilities. The Labor-Management Group, October 1983.

Codisposal of Garbage And Sewage Sludge: A Promising Solution To Two Problems. Government Accounting Office, May 1979.

Hard Choices, A Report on the Increasing Gap Between America's Infrastructure Needs and Our Ability to Pay for Them. Joint Economic Committee Report. U.S. Congress, February 25, 1984.

Urban Park and Recreation Recovery Program Impact Report, 1928-1983. Department of the Interior, National Park Service, December 1983.

Motor Vehicle Facts and Figures, 1983 edition. Motor Vehicle Manufacturers Association of the U.S., New York.

Changes in the Future Use and Characteristics of the Automobile Transportation System. Office of Technology Assessment Report, 1979.

Budget of the U.S. Government, fiscal year 1986. Executive Office of the President, Office of Management and Budget.

International Responsibilities

United Nations Demographic Yearbook, 1981, 34th issue. Department of International Economic and Social Affairs, United Nations, New York.

World Development Report, 1984. World Bank, Washington, D.C.

Jolly, Alison. A World Like Our Own: Man and Nature in Madagascar. Yale University Press, New Haven, 1980.

Hearne, Shelly. Harvest of Unknowns. Natural Resources Defense Council, New York, 1984.

Pesticide Contamination of Imported Flowers. Morbidity and Mortality Weekly Report, April 29, 1977. CDC-77-8017. Department of Health, Education and Welfare, Washington, D.C.

Mitchell, Barbara and Tinker, Jon. Antarctica and its Resources. Earthscan, London, 1980.

The Siren, No. 14. United Nations Environment Programme, Geneva, Switzerland, January 1983.

Annual Report of the Executive Director, United Nations Environment Programme. Nairobi, Kenya, May 1983.

Hazardous Waste Storage and Disposal, United Nations Environment Programme Regional Seas Reports and Studies. United Nations Environment Programme, Nairobi, Kenya, 1984.

Convention on the Prevention of Marine Pollution from Dumping of Waste and Other Matter, Annex 1. London, 1975.

Federal Trade Report 990. U.S. Department of Commerce, Bureau of Census. December, 1983.

Budgets of the Department of State, fiscal years 1980-1984. U.S. Government Printing Office.

State of the World, 1985. A Worldwatch Institute Report on Progress Toward a Sustainable Society. W. W. Norton, New York.

The Toxic Substances Control Act, 151 U.S.C. Section 2611 et seq.

The Global 2000 Report to the President. Vols. I and II. A Report Prepared by the Council on Environmental Quality and the Department of State. Barney, Gerald O., Study Director. Blue Angel, Inc., Charlottesville, VA, July 1981.

AVAILABLE FROM ISLAND PRESS

WATER IN THE WEST
VOL. I. WHAT INDIAN WATER MEANS TO
    THE WEST $15.00
VOL. II. WATER FOR THE ENERGY MARKET $15.00
VOL. III. WESTERN WATER FLOWS TO THE CITIES $25.00

By The Western Network

An essential reference tool for water managers, public officials, farmers, attorneys, industry officials, and students and professors attempting to understand the competing pressures on our most important natural resource—water. This 3-volume series provides an indepth analysis of the effects of energy development, Indian rights and urban growth on other water users.

COMMUNITY OPEN SPACES, by Mark Francis, Lisa Cashdan, Lynn Paxson. $24.95, Cloth.

Over the past decade, thousands of community gardens and parks have been developed on vacant neighborhood land in America's major cities. *Community Open Spaces* documents this movement in the U.S. and Europe, explaining how planners, public officials, and local residents can work in their own community to successfully develop open space.

PRIVATE OPTIONS: TOOLS AND CONCEPTS FOR LAND CONSERVATION, by The Montana Land Reliance and the Land Trust Exchange. $25.00. Paper.

Techniques and strategies for saving the family farm are presented by 30 experts. *Private Options* details the proceedings of a national conference and brings together, for the first time, the experience and advice of land conservation experts from all over the nation.

THE CONSERVATION EASEMENTS IN CALIFORNIA, by Thomas S. Barrett, and Putnam Livermore for the Trust for Public Land. $44.95, Cloth; $24.95, Paper.

The authoritative legal handbook on conservation easements. This book examines the California law as a model for the nation. It emphasizes the effectiveness and flexibility of the California code. Also covered are the historical and legal backgrounds of easement technology, the state and federal tax implications, and solutions to the most difficult drafting problems.

BUILDING AN ARK. TOOLS FOR THE PRESERVATION OF NATURAL DIVERSITY THROUGH LAND PROTECTION, by Phillip M. Hoose. Illustrations. $12.00, Paper.

The author, the Nature Conservancy's national protection planner, presents a comprehensive plan to identify and protect each state's natural ecological diversity. Shows how plant and animal species can be saved from destruction without penalty to landowner. Case studies augment this blueprint for conservation.

LAND-SAVING ACTION, edited by Russell L. Brenneman and Sarah M. Bates. $39.95, Cloth; $24.95, Paper.

The definitive guide for conservation practitioners. A written symposium by the 29 leading experts in land conservation. This book presents in detail land-saving tools and techniques which have been perfected by individuals and organizations across the nation. This is the first time such information has been available in one volume.

These titles are available directly from ISLAND PRESS, Order Department, Star Route 1, Box 38, Covelo, CA 95428. Please enclose $1.50 with each order for postage and handling; California residents add 6% sales tax.

About ISLAND PRESS

ISLAND PRESS is a nonprofit organization dedicated to the publication of books for professionals and concerned citizens on the conservation and management of natural resources and the environment.

Additional information and a catalog of current and forthcoming titles are available free of charge from ISLAND PRESS, 1718 Connecticut Avenue, NW Suite 300-A, Washington, D.C. 20009.